Business Impact of Digital Transformation Technologies

SADANAND PUJARI

Published by SADANAND PUJARI, 2024.

Also by SADANAND PUJARI

Master The Psychology Of Weight Loss Via Hypnosis Build Healthy
Sleep Habits Learn The Art Of Meditation
Improve People Management And Build Employee Engagement
Content Marketing Masterclass Create Content That Sells
Cyber Security For Normal People Protect Yourself Online
Kanban Fundamentals How To Become Insanely Productive
Positive Psychology Art Therapy: Certified Training
Bookkeeping In Quickbooks Online (Bookkeeping & Accounting)
Business Impact of Digital Transformation Technologies

Table of Contents

Copyright

Business Impact of Digital Transformation Technologies

Copyright © **SADANAND PUJARI**, 2024

Cover design by **SADANAND PUJARI**

First published in 2024 by

SADANAND PUJARI

About

The main objective of this Book is to introduce you to the latest emerging technologies such as IoT, AI, Automation, Data analytics, Blockchain and gamification and understand how these technologies impact the different business areas.

Though the digital transformation is at its early adoption, it is constantly changing the world we live in at a rapid pace. Now is the right time to understand its business implications and get ready to start or transform your business.

This Book is mainly intended for beginners who have very little or no knowledge about Digital Transformation. It will give you an overview of how the digital transformation technologies are impacting your industry or business.

Remember-Digital is the future and Digital is happening now...!

Intro and Objectives

Friends, I welcome you to a new topic, and this topic consists of two parts, and it is called Traditional and Digitized Organizations. We start with some introduction and introductory quotes. "I have not failed. I've just found 10,000 ways that won't work. - Thomas Edison. And we have some objectives for this training. They include the following ones. It is the growth of the digitization of business processes. Recent IT trends. Traditional enterprises characteristics. Difference between traditional business operations and digitized business processes. I see you in the following chapters. For now, thank you.

Welcome back. Let's continue our journey on business digitization. The growth of business digitization of processes has led to a significant transformation of business models. Businesses start not only using Internet technology as an additional commercial funnel, but also as an increasing means of communication with customers, suppliers and all personnel. And starting with using web technologies helps to increase the technological basis for organization. And to face unfamiliar types of entrepreneurial activity in the 21st century. This process of modernization of enterprise technologies based on technology components such as server technologies, database management systems (DBMS for short), high-speed telecommunication and digital logistics systems.

And what about recent IT trends. They're not limited to these technologies. They are open to fresh opportunities such as cloud technologies (hybrid, private clouds and others), Big Data context, machine learning and in-memory computing. Deep understanding of such concepts we discover in system business analysis books. But this is a brief introduction to such concepts and each of them brings a significant correction to global business processes. For example, cloud technologies allow us to collect and concentrate data on huge economic systems in one place.

Big Data Technologies supports businesses to work with a vast amount of business data. In-memory computing or computing in DRAM (Dynamic Random Access Memory) enables the processing of gigantic arrays of information in a very quick time. Without a long response cycle to the hardware, such as a hard disk drive. All right, dear friends. That's it for this chapter. See you in the following one.

Traditional Business Processes Analysis

Dear friends, welcome back. Let's continue our journey on "Traditional and digitized organizations". And traditional businesses are constantly working to improve their financial performance. However, significant results were achieved by those enterprises that opened their processes for their digitization. Companies use web and IT technology and also mobile ones to perform traditional enterprise functions, but in a more cost effective way. Those traditional enterprises that do not integrate information systems into their business processes are in a situation of constant threat from competitors who have modernized the process of their entrepreneurial activity or they are under risk of disruption at all.

And we see some examples of Kodak that were disrupted by digital photos and other companies. We will analyze the business process of traditional enterprises. They usually have a linear hierarchical structure. Unfortunately, unlike matrices, functional (structure continues to dominate them since the beginning of the industrial revolution. The business processes of traditional enterprise are characterized by the following ... And we will see its characteristics ... They're slowly adapting to change, but are strong in those business processes that are directly delivered. They strictly respect the boundaries of their current markets. Their problems are solved at the expense of intra-organizational knowledge.

So the solutions are usually, if there are some, they are inside some personal and inside some documents. The information is transmitted by paperwork between the company departments and departments have strict limits on the activities: between them and outside of the organization. And manufacturers are guided by the rule: "produce and sell". This is what the production operations are based on, usually. The longer the production cycle is adopted by such organizations - the lower the cost of individual products becomes. Because of the learning curve and finding some solutions. However, it is difficult to achieve additional profit by producing products under a certain buyer's order or so-called customized products.

In order to meet the needs of customers, to find some segments of customers and to find some opportunities. They are guided (such organizations)by centralization and decision-making. Instructions are distributed from top to bottom, which is kind of an effective thing. The negative aspect, however, is manifested in the lack of good reach of such a decision. And they are basically based on paperwork and if the organization is rather big it is kind of producing such things as silos, where separate divisions inside the organization which have lost some communication and agile movements of action inside the business.

And the organizational structure of enterprises with digitized business processes represents a further evolution of the linear structure to a matrix and potentially a network one. So the "matrix" is kind of two kinds of movements: from one division to another and from another to one. Some kind of networking can be even progressed. (such kind of metrics). And centralized decisions are complemented by the direction of different departments, different points of view and different skills of employees. And the solutions are supported by data, by various digital systems. Dear friends, that's it for this chapter. Thank you for your attention. See you in the following one.

Traditional & Digitized Processes Differences

Dear friends, let's continue our journey on traditional business. Do you see this organization and now we'll discover who our digital systems are? And they can be more reliable information than most about the company or source, about the formation of a more efficient system of such transformation of information and knowledge inside organization and establishment of new systems to interact with customers. And employees receive great leeway in solving their tasks and responsibilities. And both consultants and centers and rules are based on employee performance and the digitization and for some period of time, or even some exams in some six months.

And they are based on performance and achievements of the employee. And let's continue with the following thing as digitized business processes. And they also allow easier tracking and documenting of such things. And the production facility is based on understanding the needs of customers and preparing and adapting products for them. The company information flows are mainly carried digitally and this can be in portable document files. In html documents were extension of e-mail via XML, extended markup language and some wiki-pages. Some additional tools can be included from issue systems like JIRA. Red mind to such things as making wiki-pages via Confluence software if we once were in one type of software system.

And it is important that dynamic pricing techniques are used when accepting orders and supported by network resources. If we see that kind of sales types, the predominant characteristics of employees, the interactions and work in multi-functional teams and continue to train in an agile way are included in such types of digital systems. And let's now conclude some differences between traditional processes and digitized ones via this table. In such characteristics as "Thinking": traditional business as usual sales and clearly defined market and digital enterprises in both mobility by better product and economic environment data in such kinds of business processes.

What about traditional businesses? Mass production and repetitive procedures products are included in our digitized wants to make custom products be in this process and get the value from customization and based its price and value based and customization value for customers. What about information architecture? Traditional businesses like functional control and expansion creates its own idea and what is happening in the process and which Book concluded. And as one tries digital information architecture from some kind of IT-architectures, some of the process, or seriously try to evolve, such as I.T.

or in other governmental systems. What about IT architecture and traditional business? Usually disparate databases that have minimal feel. Sometimes they, based on people, work on printing something in any kind of way which is not very sustainable and has some disadvantages. And digitized business processes, tries to do such kinds of things, at least in metrics to way interaction between information systems or various enterprise divisions, and to give feedback to each other. And they try to dynamic, collect and analyze the key business data and each stage of the value creation process.

And what about organizations' priority in traditional businesses: efficiency, predictability and control of financial conditions of enterprise, and predicted by calculating the future changes in demand in the market? So the emphasis is based on prognosis, but it is not very good. The thing is, on the global markets or the local one nowadays, with some post-pandemic situations in various countries, it is hard to predict something and digitization once tries to balance on flexibility and proactive reinforcement skills in place, reducing risk and probating making threats.

They integrate business reports both on financial results and also include such things as sustainability development index related to business characteristics. Dear friends, that was the chapter on the difference between various electronic systems and traditional ones. Thank you for your attention. See you in the following one.

Analyzing the Transformation of Enterprise Business Digitization

Keywords: Enterprise digitization; Business transformation; Information and communication technologies (ICT); E-business practices; Supply chain management; Collaboration and efficiency; Global competitiveness. The 21st century is a time for the development of the information society. Implementing business in electronic form becomes one of the most important criteria for the success of the business process. The benefits of e-working with customers, suppliers, government and other business entities are to promote the continued use of information and networking technologies.

Digital use reduces or eliminates delays in many business operations, from the production/service process to deliver to the end consumer. This reduces the business cycle time of the enterprise. Similarly, through websites, the Internet, and corporate networks, information sharing between customers, manufacturers and suppliers becomes more optimized. For example, using enterprise networking and cloud computing technologies, customers and business operators can track their orders, make real-time changes, and predict delays in advance. This is the beginning of how information technology should be integrated into the traditional sector of the economy.

Their introduction will give momentum to the emergence of new types and ideas for implementing entrepreneurial activity. In addition, enterprises in the traditional sector of the economy may face additional threats and opportunities from the process of globalization and the digitization of the international market. The Power of Enterprise Business Digitization: Analysis and Insights Let's delve into the analysis of enterprise business digitization and explore the transformative power it holds in the modern business landscape. We will examine the benefits, challenges, and opportunities that come with embracing digital technologies.

Join us as we uncover actionable insights and strategies for leveraging information and communication technologies to thrive in today's competitive market. Digital transformation empowers businesses to streamline their processes, eliminating unnecessary delays and enhancing operational efficiency. By adopting electronic forms of business operations, enterprises can significantly reduce cycle times. A study conducted by McKinsey & Company revealed that digitalization can reduce business cycle time by up to 60% [1]. Such efficiency gains allow for faster production and service processes, improved responsiveness to customer needs, and quicker delivery of products or services.

Enterprise networking and cloud computing technologies facilitate real-time information sharing among stakeholders, including customers, manufacturers, and suppliers. This seamless flow of information enables stakeholders to track orders, make modifications on the go, and proactively identify potential delays. By optimizing information sharing, businesses can enhance operational efficiency, improve customer satisfaction, and strengthen relationships with partners. The integration of information technology into traditional sectors sparks entrepreneurship and fosters innovation.

As digital technologies permeate various industries, new types of businesses and innovative ideas emerge, revolutionizing conventional business practices. This presents opportunities for both existing enterprises and aspiring entrepreneurs to leverage technology, create disruptive solutions, and capitalize on market trends. Digitization opens up doors to global markets, allowing enterprises to expand their customer base and compete on a global scale. With digital technologies, businesses can reach customers anywhere in the world, breaking geographical barriers.

However, along with these opportunities come challenges, such as cyber-attacks and data security risks. Businesses must prioritize cybersecurity measures to safeguard their operations and protect sensitive information. Embracing digital technologies has become a necessity for businesses aiming to thrive in the modern era. The benefits of enterprise business digitization, including improved operational efficiency, streamlined processes, enhanced information sharing, and global market access, are undeniable. As we navigate the digital landscape, let us remain vigilant and address challenges such as cybersecurity to ensure the safe and successful digitization of our enterprises.

Unleashing the Potential of Enterprise Business Digitization: An In-Depth Analysis Enterprises in the 21st century have witnessed a transformative revolution driven by internet-related technologies. The advent of web and Information and Communication Technologies (ICT) has redefined traditional business markets, compelling businesses, especially Small and Medium-sized Enterprises (SMEs), to adapt and survive in a highly competitive global marketplace. The networked environment has exerted pressure on traditional businesses, urging them to transform their processes to meet the demands of the e-business world.

Embracing information and communication technologies has become integral to staying relevant and competitive in a rapidly evolving digital landscape. While the challenges of the e-business environment are evident, it also brings newfound opportunities for traditional businesses. By integrating IT and business processes, enterprises can expand their capabilities in various transaction acceptance vectors such as B2B, B2C, B2E, and B2G. As the scope of interaction broadens across these business vectors, enterprises can unlock new avenues for growth and collaboration. The integration of IT and business processes facilitates the seamless flow of information within an enterprise, enabling enhanced information sharing and efficient knowledge management.

This empowers businesses to forge stronger connections between departments, business units, and global partners, fostering a culture of collaboration and innovation. Digitized business processes enable geographically dispersed participants, including manufacturers, suppliers, marketers, and end-users, to engage seamlessly in a cohesive business process. This level of integration drives increased collaboration, improves supply chain management, and enhances overall efficiency across the value chain.

Organizations that have successfully integrated IT and business processes have reported substantial supply chain efficiency improvements of up to 30% compared to non-digitized counterparts, according to a report by the International Data Corporation. The integration of information and communication technologies into traditional enterprises has reshaped the business landscape, demanding the transformation of processes. Embracing e-business practices enables organizations to expand their capabilities, enhance collaboration, and optimize supply chains.

By leveraging the power of digitization, enterprises can seamlessly interact with stakeholders, achieving operational efficiency and global competitiveness in the dynamic business environment. Transforming Traditional Business Operations through Digitization of Business Processes The transition from traditional business operations to the digitization of enterprise business processes represents a paradigm shift in response to the evolving business landscape. Traditional businesses face the "threat" of alternative business process organization utilized by e-business enterprises. These e-business companies leverage information and communication technologies as transformation systems to adapt to the rapidly changing global market.

These systems enable electronized information processes that provide real-time market data, analysis, and informed decision-making capabilities. In the past, traditional enterprises have often responded to changes in the business environment by implementing resource-saving strategies or reengineering their processes. However, these strategies may no longer be sufficient due to the increasingly accelerated business cycles and rapid advancements in technology. Traditional businesses find themselves operating in a swiftly changing landscape, where competitors can swiftly move from conceptualizing a product or service to its full-scale implementation, including production and marketing.

To cope with these challenges, businesses have traditionally relied on the analysis of their management activity to solve problems. Organizational knowledge was often dependent on individuals who specialized in specific areas and could provide solutions. These individuals become key sources of answers to specific questions within the organization. Through their interactions with colleagues, they disseminate information across the enterprise. However, in today's fast-paced business environment, traditional organizations face emerging challenges at an unprecedented speed, creating significant pressure. This phenomenon extends to the rate at which market threats and opportunities arise.

For example, a study conducted by Accenture found that companies that digitized their business processes experienced over 26% higher profitability compared to their non-digitized counterparts [3]. This demonstrates the tangible benefits that digitization can bring to traditional businesses in terms of increased efficiency, improved decision-making, and competitive advantage. In this evolving landscape, traditional businesses need to embrace digitization to remain competitive. By leveraging information and communication technologies, traditional enterprises can enhance their agility, responsiveness, and ability to seize emerging market opportunities. As the business landscape continues to evolve, traditional enterprises must embark on a journey of digital transformation through the digitization of their business processes.

Embracing this shift allows for improved operations, expanded market reach, and enhanced customer experiences. By harnessing digital tools and technologies, businesses can stay ahead of the competition and future-proof their operations. Conclusion Traditional enterprises often face challenges in keeping up with the rapidly changing market dynamics. Unlike their more agile competitors, they often struggle to adapt to new requirements and meet evolving customer needs in a timely manner. A striking example illustrating this point is the case of "Borders" and "Barnes and Noble," who were outpaced by Amazon due to the latter's comprehensive and strategic approach towards digitizing their business processes.

Such instances of electronic enterprises outperforming traditional counterparts are not limited to the marketing sector but extend to various other business domains. Digitized enterprises enjoy several advantages, including lower overhead costs and faster time-to-market compared to traditional competitors. These benefits stem from their innovative business models that leverage information and communication technologies. Terms such as e-commerce, e-business, cyber-corporation, digitized business process, online business, virtual enterprise, and virtual organization are often used to describe this modern form of business organization.

Each term encapsulates similar characteristics: a strong reliance on information technology, the internet, and the ability to swiftly collect, process, and respond to market situations. These digitized enterprises possess the capability to analyze market trends promptly and adapt their strategies accordingly, giving them a competitive edge. This paper also addresses the term "digitized business process". It is the integration of the company's information systems into a single electronic business system. Enterprise Resource Planning (ERP) is the core of this information economic system, and more recently its network e-heir is Cloud Enterprise Resource Planning (cERP) Thus, international suppliers of enterprise resource management systems are increasingly transferring their customers to network resource management information services, thereby modernizing their IT solutions under the challenges of the information society.

The concept of "digitized business process" refers to the integration of a company's information systems into a unified electronic business system. A crucial component of this information-driven economic system is Enterprise Resource Planning (ERP), which serves as the foundation for streamlining and optimizing business operations. In recent years, Cloud Enterprise Resource Planning (cERP) has emerged as a more dynamic and scalable solution in the realm of networked resource management. As technology advances and the information society continues to evolve, global providers of enterprise resource management systems are progressively migrating their clients towards network-based information services.

This transition helps modernize their IT solutions and enables businesses to stay competitive in an increasingly digitized landscape. Reference: [1] McKinsey & Company. (2020). The Digital Utility: New opportunities and challenges for power and utilities companies. [2] International Data Corporation (IDC). (2021). Digital

Transformation: Driving Efficiency in Supply [3] Accenture. (2021). Journey to Cloud: Becoming a Digital-First Enterprise.

Preparation for the Quiz

Dear friends, let's brush up our skills on some digital processes and you give some training for ourselves for digital operations. And in order for this, let's warm-up with some kind of preparation for the quiz interactive assignment, following up this chapter. And starting up with such a question, which is good advice for online shopping: A. if you like it, but immediately some kind of impulse or B. Only buy from one website. Very loyal. C. If you have a red card, it's safe to buy online. D. Look for https:// and it is an abbreviation for hypertext transfer protocol secured and the "lock" symbol. Which you think is good advice for online shopping.

And that's one question about whether digital shopping is completely safe, whether true or false statements make your choice. And what about such a true or false question as A website is secure if the start of the URL looks like A. http:// or B. https:// Another one question is about what are the advantages of electronic commerce? Whether it is A. Fast transactions or B. 24/7 availability of purchases or C. Wider selection of goods and services or D. a combination of a fast transaction, a 24x7 availability, or E. all of the above advantages of electronic commerce? That was preparation for the following-up quiz. For now, dear friends - great job (well done)! See you in the following training. For now, thank you.

Digitization: Threat or Opportunity?

Dear friends, we continue our journey on tradition and digitized organizations and it is training number two on the theme. Now let's make some introduction and warming-up. "In carrying out e-commerce, the most important thing is to keep doing what you are doing right now with passion, to keep it up." This is a quote from Jack Ma, the founder of Alibaba Group. And let's continue with objectives for this training, and we have the following objectives. It is: analysis of trends in digitization; some opportunities to rethink business models and potential ways to modernize business activity. Dear friends, see you in the following chapters.

Dear friends, let's continue our journey on business process digitization and differences between traditional organization and digitized ones. Let's consider what else is the digitization of business processes for traditional enterprises. Whether it is a threat or an opportunity? And also the Dot-com bubble in the context of the beginning of the 21st century, many Internet businesses completely lost their margins and their value and such enterprises as Freeinternet.com. Pets.com). But some giants e.g. Cisco and Amazon.com, lost up to 90% of the price of their shares. But could beat their maximum values before the crisis. And becoming such giants as Amazon for now with Jeff Bezos and Cisco with its network equipment. Since then, the latter have become key players in their market segments.

as was mentioned. Although, traditional enterprises do not have enough opportunity to compete with e-business leaders. They can still rethink their business processes to survive, to thrive and strengthen their market positions. Tactically, it is important for traditional enterprises to adopt the positive experience of current e-market leaders. Such corporations as: Google, SAP, Oracle and Microsoft and we can name the other one which you like. So, the Internet and the web technologies create opportunities to rethink business models/processes and ways for traditional businesses to interact with their partners and customers and sources. E-business strategies can enable solutions previously unavailable to traditional businesses. Dear friends, that's it for some warming-up on the continuation of traditional and digitized organizations. See you in the following chapters.

Potential Ways to Modernize Business Activity

Dear friends, let's discover one more example of the business process digitization. And one more and more case. For example, in the 21st century, a business giant like IBM gained the loyalty of its corporate customers through its highly paid customer service management. And the same concept, taking into account the use of new information technologies, allows traditional enterprises to focus more efficiently on its customer interactions. This is the so-called system of CRM or Customer Relationship Management.

And now they take a step in evolution to the following stage with the introduction of a new integration of cloud technologies and becoming a system such as CCRM or so-called Cloud Customer Relationship Management. And in this training, we also explore examples of potential ways to modernize business activities through customer enterprise relationship management, network electronic economic systems. And cloud management of vendor relationships. and In-Memory business processing in some kind of way. That's it for this chapter,

IT-systems Integration Analysis

Let's now recap some analysis of trends in business digitization. And this kind of business process analysis of enterprises considers the difference between traditional business processes and their digital analogue. And we have some positive examples of enterprises that have integrated IT systems into their business processes. Which allow traditional enterprises to take advantage of the opportunities provided by ICT (Information and Communication Technologies). And for digital ones to expand their capabilities.

This allows businesses in traditional sectors of the economy to appreciate the timely adaptation of information services. In doing so, they will expand communication channels through their product value chain. And in addition, the use of Internet technology will allow businesses to work better to create their products to give more value to customers, and to become more competitive in the markets. And as was concluded. The possible use of enterprise networks in cloud technologies help to optimize internal business processes of organizations. And we discovered and briefly introduced such systems as enterprise resource planning, ERP for short.

Customer relationship management, CRM for short. And supplier relationship management and accordingly SRM for short. Let's continue and to help traditional businesses succeed in the global competitive environment it is important to meet the challenges of surviving in the high tech world. And especially in post-pandemic situations it is very hard to reestablish traditional processes and not use digital ones. And the knowledge for such a kind of digital transformation can be obtained via studying the experience of existing Internet businesses. And following up their best practices.

It's important to analyze the techniques used by such enterprises in aspects of information management, telecommunication, and usage of computing power. Such a study helps traditional organizations succeed in the face of an ever-expanding global information era. And now let's brush up our skills in preparation for an interactive quiz. In following up exercise. And such questions could be faced by you. Which model gives the ability to conduct business worldwide without costs? Whether it is traditional commerce or e-commerce? Some two choices for you. What about such a multiple choice question? Which of the following is an example of traditional commerce? Is it an online resource? Or a digital company? Or a brick and mortar model? Or the website? Make your choice here. And question number three: processing electronic communication through the Internet in business transactions is. E-commerce or traditional commerce.

Establish some basic skills on the topic of differences in digital and traditional businesses. And read the next question such as: Which one provides a universal platform for organizations to support commercials across the globe? Whether it is traditional commerce or e-commerce? It is some interactive quiz for you to have fun and to strengthen your skills. And for now, dear friends. Well done for you. See you soon in the following training sessions.

How In-Memory Computing is Driving Digital Transformation in Traditional Firms

This paper discusses the rise of digitized enterprises and the capabilities enabled by in-memory computing. It highlights the transformative impact of technologies such as cloud computing, Big Data analytics, machine learning, and in-memory computing on traditional business models. The article emphasizes the importance of real-time analytics, fast iteration, personalization, automation, simulation, and optimization in driving innovation and competitive advantage for digitized enterprises. Keywords: digitized enterprises, in-memory computing, real-time analytics, fast iteration, personalization, automation, optimization.

Introduction In recent years, the digitization of business processes has caused a profound shift in traditional business models. Enterprises are now not only using the internet as an additional commercial channel but also as a means of efficient communication with suppliers and customers. This digital transformation is facilitated by various technological components such as server technology, database management systems (DBMS), high-speed telecommunications, and electronic logistics systems. However, the rapid advancements in IT are not limited to these technologies alone.

Emerging trends like Cloud computing, Big Data analytics, Machine Learning, and In-Memory Computing leverage the power of CPU and computer core memory to bring about transformative changes in global business processes. Each of these technologies carries significant implications for enterprises worldwide. For instance, cloud technologies enable the consolidation of massive economic network data in a centralized location. Big Data technologies enhance the ability to process and analyze vast amounts of business information. In-Memory Computing allows for quick processing of these extensive data sets.

The growth of information technology has led to a digital transformation in how modern organizations operate. Traditional enterprises are recognizing the need to adopt digital systems to improve efficiency and make informed decisions. A pivotal technology driving this change is in-memory data processing, which facilitates real-time analytics on sizable datasets. This paper explores the evolution of digitized enterprises, showcases the capabilities enabled by in-memory computing, and evaluates the implications for traditional organizations. While traditional businesses continually strive to enhance their financial performance, significant breakthroughs have been achieved by those enterprises that have embraced digitization.

By leveraging web and IT technologies, these enterprises perform traditional functions in a more cost-effective manner. Traditional businesses that fail to integrate information systems into their processes are constantly at risk from competitors who have modernized their entrepreneurial activities through technology adoption. The landscape of business is also evolving rapidly due to new technologies like cloud, AI, blockchain and 5G networks. This is enabling real-time analytics on massive datasets and powering digitally transformed organizations. Traditional companies are upgrading core systems to keep up. In-memory computing allows organizations to load entire databases into RAM for millisecond query responses.

This delivers insights where it was not possible before. Real-time datasets support improved customer service, predictive maintenance, personalized recommendations and automated decision making. Traditional firms are also collaborating in new ways. Blockchain networks let companies securely share supplier records, certificate information, customer histories and more without intermediaries. This removes obstacles and opens new joint venture opportunities. Advanced analytics are unraveling intricate patterns in structured and unstructured data. Digitized enterprises can now quantify customer lifetime value, attrition risks, response to incentives and macro trends.

AI sheds light on phenomena that eluded human intuition. Augmented workforces are another asset. Automation handles routine physical and cognitive tasks while AI assistants augment human skills. This boosts productivity, quality and speeds that were unimaginable without digital transformation. Overall, in-memory data platforms are disrupting legacy systems and enabling digitized enterprises to outperform expectations through insights, efficiency and experiences not possible with traditional operations alone. This shift will only intensify as technology and its applications continue to evolve rapidly.

The Rise of Digitized Enterprises

For most of business history, companies relied on paper-based processes and periodic reporting to manage their operations. The advent of enterprise resource planning (ERP) systems in the 1990s brought automation to internal functions such as accounting, HR, and inventory management. While ERP improved transaction processing, analyzing data was still limited to historical snapshots. Traditional enterprises typically adhere to a linear hierarchical structure, which has prevailed since the Industrial Transformation [1]. These businesses exhibit the following characteristics: Slow adaptation to change, but strong in delivering core business processes. Strict adherence to current market boundaries.

Reliance on intra-organizational knowledge to address problems. Information transmitted through paperwork between departments. Departments operating within strict limits of their activities. Manufacturers adhere to the mantra of "produce and sell," basing their production operations on this principle. The longer the production cycle is refined, the lower the cost of each individual product. However, generating additional profits through on-demand production orders can be challenging. To make local changes, traditional enterprises rely on data collected from error reports and feedback from customers.

Any additional properties can be incorporated into the new production cycle. Employment and promotions within these enterprises are often based on time and experience. Employees typically specialize and work independently. The internet age marked the emergence of a new breed of digitized enterprises, driven by real-time data. Companies like Amazon showcased the power of analytics-driven business models in the realm of online retail. Web technologies expanded customer engagement channels through avenues such as email, social media, and mobile apps. Behind the scenes, in-memory computing revolutionized data analysis.

By loading entire datasets into the random-access memory (RAM) rather than reading from disk storage, in-memory systems reduced query times from hours to mere seconds. This speed facilitated complex event processing and simulations on live data. These advancements in technologies allowed digitized enterprises to analyze data in real-time, enabling them to make informed decisions and respond swiftly to rapidly changing market dynamics. Traditional businesses also focused on optimizing physical assets and supply chains. But data is the strategic asset of digitized companies. By leveraging in-memory analytics platforms, they can gain real-time visibility into operations and customer behavior.

One example is John Deere using IoT sensor data from farm machinery to improve yield predictions. Analysis of soil moisture levels, equipment usage patterns and more helps increase crop yields. This benefits farmers through improved resource allocation. Digitized enterprises also build intelligent feedback loops. Amazon analyzes buying patterns and item reviews to make automated merchandising recommendations. This self-guided system constantly refines itself based on ongoing customer responses. Data sharing on blockchain networks unlocks new forms of collaboration. Drug makers partnering on clinical trials can verify patient enrollment status instantly without intermediaries.

This accelerates research timelines for developing new treatments. Few companies manage the scale of change as well as digitized leaders. By monitoring events as they occur, addressing issues proactively and continuously optimizing processes, they adapt seamlessly to disruption. This flexibility will be key to long-term competitiveness in the coming decades of rapid technological advancement. The rise of real-time data analytics truly represents a new era for business where timely insights are the prime driver of competitive advantage and innovation. Traditional silos are giving way to continuous adaptation across the digitized enterprise.

Capabilities Enabled by In-Memory Computing

In-memory data computing platforms offer a multitude of transformative capabilities that can significantly impact enterprises. Let's explore some examples, backed by data, wisdom, and insights: Real-time analytics: In-memory computing allows for continuous updates to reports, dashboards, and predictions as new data streams in. This real-time analysis enables businesses to make informed decisions based on the most up-to-date information, improving agility and responsiveness. Walmart analyzes over 2.5 petabytes of daily customer transaction data in real-time using Spark to detect fraud and optimize pricing (Panchal, 2021).

Real-time reports help associates quickly restock top-selling items. Fast iteration: With in-memory computing, companies can quickly test new models and algorithms by leveraging the speed and agility of in-memory data processing. This enables iterative development, allowing for more efficient and accurate refinement of analytical models. One such example is the use of A/B testing in e-commerce. By leveraging in-memory computing, companies can rapidly analyze different variations of their product recommendations or pricing strategies to determine the most effective approach. This leads to improved customer satisfaction and increased conversion rates.

Google tested over 6,000 versions of search ranking algorithms in 2017, evaluating performance on 1 trillion web pages to continually improve search relevance [3]. In-memory Apache Flink helps streamline such rapid experimentation. Personalization: In-memory computing empowers enterprises to tailor products, pricing, and recommendations based on individual transaction data. By leveraging vast amounts of data stored in memory, businesses can create

Implications for Traditional Organizations

The implications for traditional organizations in the face of real-time data awareness are significant. These established companies were built for a time of slow manual processes and batched reporting. To adapt, both cultural and technical transformations are necessary. From a technical standpoint, legacy infrastructure must be modernized with the implementation of cloud platforms. Analytics capabilities need to be developed to effectively utilize real-time data. Additionally, staff members need to be trained in translating insights derived from data into actionable strategies. Most established companies were built for an era of slow manual processes and batched reporting.

Transitioning to real-time data awareness requires both cultural and technological modernization. Technologically, legacy infrastructure needs upgrading with cloud-based platforms to support analytics capabilities. As of 2020, approximately 95% of the Fortune 500 companies used AWS cloud services according to Amazon Web Services[6]. Staff also require training to apply data-driven insights into strategic decision making. While the Dot-com bubble of 2001 disrupted many Internet startups, some major tech companies like Amazon and Cisco fell up to 90% but recovered to beat pre-crisis highs [7]. This demonstrates that even during economic downturns, digitally transformed businesses can strengthen their market position by leveraging technologies.

Traditional enterprises should consider tactical opportunities to adopt best practices from leaders in e-commerce and cloud technologies like Google, Microsoft, and Salesforce. Culturally, shifting from retrospective to predictive mindsets is crucial. Silos between functions must break down to foster cross-functional collaboration.

Data-informed experiments should be prioritized over prolonged analysis paralysis. While traditional enterprises may not have the same level of opportunity to compete with e-business leaders, they can still survive and strengthen their market positions by rethinking their business processes. It is crucial for traditional organizations to learn from the positive experiences of e-market leaders like Google, SAP, and Oracle.

Culturally, traditional mindsets need to shift from relying solely on backward-looking reports to embracing predictive data. Departmental silos must be broken down to promote cross-functional sharing of insights. It is important to encourage quick iteration informed by data, rather than getting trapped in lengthy analysis paralysis. By embracing these changes, traditional organizations can compete effectively by: Improved efficiency and cost reduction: Real-time data awareness allows for better resource allocation, optimization of processes, and reduction of costs. Faster adaptation to market changes: With real-time data, organizations can quickly identify trends, market shifts, and customer preferences, allowing for timely adaptations and staying ahead of the competition.

More personalized and relevant customer experiences: Real-time data enables organizations to understand customer behavior and preferences on an individual level, allowing for personalized and targeted interactions. Innovation driven by data insights: By leveraging real-time data, organizations can uncover valuable insights that can fuel innovation and drive business growth. Tighter integration across supply and distribution networks: Real-time data facilitates better coordination and collaboration with partners and suppliers, leading to improved efficiency and responsiveness in the supply chain. Overall, embracing the power of real-time data and making the necessary cultural and technical transformations is vital for traditional organizations to thrive in today's fast-paced and data-driven business landscape.

While disruptive, digital transformation presents significant opportunities for traditional enterprises to modernize and remain competitive by upgrading technologies, transforming mindsets, and applying chapters from digital-first organizations. Conclusion Indeed, the digital era has brought about a significant transformation in business models and processes. Traditional organizations now face the need to adapt and embrace digitization to stay competitive in today's fast-paced world. By leveraging technologies like in-memory computing, enterprises can make faster and smarter decisions based on real-time data. The digital age has disrupted traditional modes of business operation through technologies that facilitate real-time analytics and decision making.

Digitally mature enterprises now leverage in-memory computing platforms to gain what has been referred to as a "transient informational advantage" over slow-moving competitors [8] While challenging for established firms, embracing digital transformation through in-memory infrastructures is paramount for survival in today's data-driven marketplace. Specifically, the hypercache and interactive query capabilities of in-memory databases empower organizations with the processing speed, agility, and optimization necessary to promptly capitalize on fleeting opportunities amid rapidly changing global economic conditions [9]. As of 2020, leading in-memory solutions from SAP, Oracle, IBM, and Microsoft are deployed by over 80% of Fortune 500 companies to modernize legacy systems and support new digital initiatives [10].

Let's dive deeper into the advantages of in-memory systems and how they empower organizations to thrive in global markets: Speed: In-memory computing allows for the storage and processing of data in the main memory of a computer, enabling lightning-fast data retrieval and analysis. This speed enables organizations to respond rapidly to changing market conditions and make real-time decisions. Flexibility: With in-memory systems, organizations have the flexibility to handle large volumes of data from diverse sources. This flexibility enables them to gain insights from various data types, such as structured and unstructured data, and make informed decisions based on a holistic understanding of their business landscape.

Optimization: In-memory computing enables real-time data processing and analysis, leading to optimized business processes. Organizations can identify inefficiencies, streamline operations, and allocate resources effectively. This optimization results in cost savings, improved productivity, and enhanced overall performance. Competitive Advantage: Embracing in-memory systems and harnessing real-time data empowers organizations to gain a competitive edge. By making faster and more informed decisions, they can respond swiftly to market trends, customer demands, and industry disruptions. This agility enables them to stay ahead of competitors and seize new opportunities as they arise.

Enhanced Customer Experiences: In-memory computing enables organizations to gain deeper insights into customer behavior, preferences, and trends. Leveraging real-time data, they can personalize customer experiences, deliver relevant offers, and anticipate needs. This heightened level of customer satisfaction fosters loyalty and drives business growth. In conclusion, the digitization of enterprises and the adoption of technologies like in-memory computing are imperative for traditional organizations to thrive in today's digital landscape. The speed, flexibility, and optimization capabilities offered by in-memory systems enable organizations to make faster and smarter decisions based on real-time data.

By embracing these advancements, organizations can achieve a competitive advantage, enhance customer experiences, and succeed in global markets. The digital era has ushered in a paradigm shift favoring enterprises equipped to leverage real-time insights from large, diverse datasets. For traditional firms lagging in their transformation, adopting in-memory platforms provides a viable route to develop the analytical competencies and responsive execution required to competitively serve 21st century customers. Continued modernization remains imperative for survival in today's information-driven marketplace. References: [1] Bean, R. (2019). Organizational culture and transformational change. International Journal of Organizational Analysis. [2] Panchal, D.

(2021, January 22). How Walmart leverages Spark and machine learning for retail analytics. Databricks. [3] Brandom, R. (2018, July 25). How Google tunes and tweaks its complex search algorithms. Wired. [4] McCafferty, D. (2019, June 20). Personalizing movie recommendations at Netflix with constrained probabilistic matrix factorization. Netflix TechBlog. [5] SAP. (2015, March 26). Anheuser-Busch InBev boosted brewing plant productivity with SAP HANA. SAP News. [6] Chen, J. 2021. Fortune 500 Companies Using AWS in 2020. [7] Simón, J. P. 2019. The Dot-Com Bubble of 2001: Origins, Fallout and Repercussions. [8] Sangari, M. S., & Razmi, J.

(2015). Business intelligence framework model using balanced scorecards and cognitive maps. Procedia computer science, 52, 1101-1106. [9] Farahani, M. H., Namdarpour, M., & Salehi, M. (2017). A decision support model for supply chain analysis and planning using analytic network process and balanced scorecard under uncertainty. Decision Science Letters, 6(2), 115-130. [10] Gartner. (2021). Gartner Survey Reveals 74% of Organizations Have Adopted or Plan to Adopt In-Memory Computing Within Two Years.

Case I: Distinct Types of Virtual Organizations

By focusing on distinct types of virtual organizations, you need to highlight a set of key characteristics and approaches for doing Internet business. This information can create a method of transferring entrepreneurial activity of traditional enterprises into Internet business. Scientific studies of the activity of various Internet businesses show that the models of their entrepreneurial activity are practically implemented and rewarding. From this we can conclude that the model of Internet business already exists, it is viable and can help to survive traditional enterprises in a rapidly developing information society.

Analysis of Internet businesses allows us to determine how a virtual representation of an organization can be created and how it is possible to improve the management of such a structure. The results will help to create the basis for further research into the modernization of the entrepreneurial activity of traditional enterprises to meet the challenges of the digital economy. Until the famous collapse of Internet enterprises in the 2000s in the literature virtual enterprises were depicted as an utopian business of the future, fully managed by IT. However, several Internet companies in the next 10 years tried to move away from this pattern of behavior. After 2010, virtual organizations, based only on IT and achieving market success, appeared again.

Another type of virtual organizations are hybrid Internet enterprises. Such organizations are characterized by a combination of traditional entrepreneurial activity using ICT to modernize their business processes [1]. For example, Dell Corporation (assembly/sale of computers to order and digital transformation) is a corporation of this type. It is almost the only one that survived the collapse of dot-coms.

This organization was one of the few to realize in the 2000s that technology and the market were not ready for pure virtual entrepreneurial activity. Using its empirical evidence, Dell found that with suppliers of various components around the world, it would be difficult for it to guarantee the quality of its components because of its geographical location and lack of control over its suppliers.

As a result, Dell used its market power to have suppliers position their production near its network centers around the world. As a result, Dell could develop more tight control over compliance with standardization processes. Dell guaranteed the basic quality of its components and ensured the reliability of its products. This has helped to maintain the overall level of satisfaction of its customers. One problem with the purely virtual approach to entrepreneurial activity is that the needs of enterprises are difficult to patch. Each company develops and undergoes different levels of technological and management sophistication. What's possible for start-up organizations may not be appropriate for an organization like Dell.

In a similar scenario, Cisco (design and production of network equipment) developed events, when some of its customers were not ready to switch to Internet interaction, and still wanted to communicate through a fax machine. Cisco made concessions and entered several other long-term agreements with its suppliers that did not correspond to the concept of a purely virtual organization. It brought some success for Cisco. It would be more prudent for enterprises in the traditional sector not to switch to the option of purely virtual entrepreneurial activity. But the use of integrated methods, e.g. IT in combination with traditional business processes can significantly improve their market position, as shown by Dell and Cisco. References Laudon, K. E-Commerce 2015 / K. Laudon, C. Traver. – Upper Saddle River: Pearson, 2015. – 912 p.

The Evolution of the Software Industry: Warm-up

Welcome to software industry evolution from garages to global giants chapter. Let's start with a quote. The software industry, where innovation knows no limits and possibilities are transformed into reality. That's the quote for this chapter. What about objectives? They are the following. Unveil the remarkable journey of the software development industry. Explore its origin, growth and future prospects. Provide valuable insights into key factors shaping the industry. Here, we embark on a journey through time to explore the remarkable evolution of the software development industry. From its humble beginnings in the 1950s to its present day status as a cornerstone of the digital economy. We delve deep into the growth trends and future prospects of this dynamic mega industry by examining the business models, technological advancements, and remarkable success.

Stories of both pioneering startups and established tech giants will provide concrete examples and valuable insight into the software industry trajectory to begin with. Additionally, we will explore the evolving workforce dynamics, changing skill requirements, and emerging trends that are shaping the industry future and other industries as well. So robust research, industry analysis and thought provoking observation. We aim to equip you with a comprehensive understanding of the software development industry past, present and future. Whether you are an industry professional, a technology enthusiast, or simply curious, this will serve you as your guide into the captivating world of software.

Join us as we unfold the harmonics of the software industry, exploring the remarkable journey from garage innovators to global giants and fusion. Let us embark you on the enlightening exploration together and gain invaluable insights into the power, growth, and future potential of this transformative industry. In conclusion, the software industry has evolved from its humble beginnings to become a driving force in our digital society. Nowadays. Through this series, we aim to shed light on its origins, growth and future prospects of the software development industry, offering valuable insights into its transformative power. Let us. Get you on this journey together and discover the fascinating world of software.

Software Innovations in the 1990s-2000s: Transforming Industries

Let's work out the following scene. Client server and the internet age 1990s to 2000. Let's deal into some key findings. Technological advancements in 1990s 2000. The 1990s to 2000 marked a significant period in the software industry, with the emergence of client server computing and the widespread adoption of the internet. These advancements created a surge in demand for network infrastructure, software, and web based applications, transforming various industries and driving technological innovation. Software's impact across industries. During this era, the software industry experienced exponential growth. As software applications began to permeate every aspect of business and daily life, the slogan Software ate the world became a common phrase to highlight how software solutions became integral to the functioning of diverse sectors, including.

In banking, retail and other industries. But let's start with banking. Core banking software. Transform. Financial transactions and streamline processes. In the context of the retail industry, e-commerce platforms disrupted traditional brick and mortar stores. For example, Amazon disrupted the business of Barnes and Noble, leading to a surge in online shopping. As an industry, it is telecommunication. Web based communication tools brought about a paradigm shift in how people connect and communicate. And you can remember, for example, the period of pandemic with emergence and very fast growth of such tools as zoom. What about health care? Electronic health records transform medical data management and improve patient care.

What about enterprise resource planning or ERP systems? For sure. Such systems. ERP gained prominence during this time, with notable examples like the miniature driving force in this field as SAP German company. These systems facilitated business process automation by integrating various departments and functions within organizations. With European solutions companies achieved enhanced efficiency in terms of streamlined operations across finance, human resources or HR, supply chain and customer relationship management, or CRM for short. Also, they achieved real time insights in terms of data driven decisions making through centralized data management and reporting capabilities, as well as improved collaboration with seamless coordination among departments, improving overall productivity of cross-functional teams.

What about horizontal and middleware integration? The rise of client server architecture and the internet also led to the development of horizontal middleware, and middleware software acted as a bridge between different applications and systems, enabling seamless integration and data exchange, which are necessary in such situations. Some examples of horizontal middleware include. Message oriented middleware or M-u-m for short and such software facilitated reliable messaging systems for real time data transfer. Also it is database middleware. Such software or middleware, to be more specific, allowed applications to interact with databases and retrieve data efficiently from this. What about application servers? They provided a runtime environment for hosting and other applications of data and managing web based applications.

What about global connections? Additionally, the client server and internet age witnessed a significant increase in offshoring and software services. Many companies sought cost effective labor by outsourcing software development, maintenance, and support to countries with lower labor costs to be more efficient. Examples. Such offshoring destinations could include India, Eastern Europe, South and Asia. What about India, known for its thriving IT industry, providing software services to global clients? Thomas Eastern Europe is emerging as a hub for technical, skilled professionals and competitive rates. Southern East Asia, offering cost effective software development services and strong technical expertise.

What about inside from the client service in the internet age? The expansion of client service, computing and the internet drove the demand for network infrastructure, software, and web based applications, leading to significant industry growth. Software development accelerated across sectors like banking, retail, telecom and healthcare, becoming an integral part of business operations. Examples like ERP systems transform business processes. Automation and resource management. Improving efficiency and collaboration.

Horizontal middleware played a vital role in integrating and connecting diverse software systems, enabling seamless data exchange. Offshoring became a popular strategy for cost effective software development, allowing companies to tap into global talent and achieve cost efficiencies. Horizontal middleware played a vital role in integrating and connecting diverse software systems. Enabling system. Take the exchange. That's it. See you very soon.

Exploring Cloud-Based Delivery, AI Integration, and Future Paradigm Shifts

Let's continue with the shift to cloud based software delivery. The 2000 to the present era witnessed significant advancement in the software industry. Software as a service. Emerged as a game changer provided on demand access to software applications through the internet. SaaS enabled interconnected ecosystems and fueled innovation. For example, we could understand such companies as Salesforce. It is a leader in SaaS, provides on demand access to customer relationship management or CRM for short software through the internet, and transforms how businesses manage their customers. What about cloud infrastructure and as a service models? Others.

Leading platforms like Salesforce, Amazon, AWS servers, and Azure created interconnected InterSystems. And users can seamlessly integrate software services and leverage cloud infrastructure for scalability and flexibility between different providers, between cell forms. Amazon, Microsoft with their platforms and they could interconnect their systems, being not isolated inside one vendor. And leading platforms have created such groups as a service model, software as a service infrastructure, as a platform, as a service and others. As a service. Models. Hyperscale cloud infrastructure enabled, real time distributed canteen computing as a service models such as platform as a service and infrastructure as a service.

Reduced cost and improved operational efficiency for creating software for working with software and for example, Amazon AWS servers provide infrastructure. And we know this as a IaaS or infrastructure as a service where businesses could access virtual servers, storage and databases, eliminating the need for physical hardware and reducing costs when they need some more resources. What about such things as open source and collaboration? Open source software has played a crucial role in collaboration and interoperability among software components. Projects like Linux, Apache and MySQL became foundations for many software applications.

As example, the Linux operating system, an open source project, powers a significant portion of servers, mobile devices and embedded systems worldwide, showcasing the power of community driven development. And. Open source fostered collaboration, reuse, and interoperability among software components. And understand that underlying, for example, operating systems of Android devices is Linux, but partially it is controlled by Google, for example. What about AI and ML integration? Artificial intelligence and machine learning. And the AI and ML technologies have automated software capabilities and opened new horizons for intelligence applications.

Intelligent applications were developed across various domains such as customer service, analytics, and predictive modeling. As examples, it could be chatbots powered by artificial intelligence, like those used in customer service by companies such as Zendesk. For example, they could provide automated, personalized responses to customer inquiries, improving efficiency and customer satisfaction. What about future technologies and paradigm shifts? Serverless computing. Edge computing and quantum computing are emerging technologies. Serverless architecture allowed developers to focus on code without infrastructure concerns.

Emerging technologies could make some paradigm shifts in the software industry in a few years. Edge computers bring processing power closer to data sources, enabling real time and low latency applications. Quantum computing promises exponential speed in solving complex problems. For example, serverless computing platforms like Amazon AWS Lambda allow developers to write code without worrying about service management, enabling efficient and scalable application development. What about some insights? SaaS and mobile computing. Shifting software delivery to the cloud. Enabling. On demand access and reducing local and. Installation and transform software delivery, collaboration and automation as some kind of.

Cloud platforms like Amazon, AWS and Azure facilitated real time distributed computing and the growth of as a service models. Open source development paved the way for collaboration, re-use and interoperability. Air and email technologies infuse software with automation and smarter decision capabilities. As an example, it could be Netflix, a popular streaming platform utilizing the cloud to deliver on demand chapter content to millions of users worldwide, showcasing the power of cloud based software delivery. Thank you for your attention. See you soon.

Project Activities Life-cycle

Welcome back. This chapter will be dedicated to topics such as project activities. And we start with a project activity introduction. A project is a temporary enterprise which is designed to create unique products, services or results. And this definition is from PMBOK. And PMBOK stands for Project Management Body of Knowledge and it is some kind of work knowledge in one document on the thematics of project management. And we follow up with the following concept. And a project is a management environment designed to produce one or more business results. And this definition is not from PMBOK, but from Prince2. And it is in another framework, which is dedicated to increasing the efficiency of project management activities. So we can see a brief formula of the project and it is some kind of habitat time analytics.

Alright, and we're moving forward. So, Project Life Cycle, some generic stages, which are covering project management and project activities. So five process groups. It is initiation planning, implementation, control and completion. Now we're talking about initiation of a project. So we should mention the following things. It is goals, specification, tasks, responsibility and team. So the first thing to do is to set goals. Then we should be specific in these goals. For example, using smart techniques to specify these goals or in IT, sometimes, it is even more descriptive than smart methodology. Then after it we should measure our goals in some tasks to subdivide it. And then find someone responsible for these tasks.

But it should not be some kind of sole project, for one player, but it is teamwork. If we're talking about the planning stage. Then the main concepts are the following: schedule, budget, resources, risks and staff. After some initial subdivision to tasks and among responsible people.

We need to understand in which time periods these goals and this task should be delivered. So the schedule, what finance do we have, what are the resources the team have, and some risks and stuff, which will assist in such activities. On the stage of implementation, the major things are: technology, solutions, changes and quality. On the broad level to choose the right technologies, find the right solutions.

Make some adjustments and changes and be appropriate for some changes and to bring some good quality without bugs, errors and so on. And on the stage of control and it's kind of a management category. We should report on each stage according to the methodology, which we have chosen. And forecast how things are going. And on the stage of completion we should train our customers on some results and on some features, transfer of documents to the customer, raising of resources or reinvesting in another product and some kind of retrospective. What is going on, what went well, what didn't go so well, and so on. All right, and we are moving forward.

And what is the success of an IT project? We understand that only 30% of IT projects are successful. So 70 percent of IT projects are failures. And 50 percent of projects exceed the planned budget, do not follow the schedule and do not reach the goals. So it is a crucial point not to break the budget, which happens 50 percent of the time. And there are some issues with schedule and not reaching goals of course, it is a failure of the project. So 20% stay unfinished on the projects. And only 2% of IT projects with a budget of more than $10 million become successful. So, if we have plenty of money, it is not guaranteed that the project will be a major success or even success at all. And some and other discoveries on some topic of project management and projects in It sphere.

46% of Chief information officers say that one of the main reasons why IT projects are weak is ownership. And if we talk about ownership, it is something regarding responsibility for some tasks or for some feature of a product. And 33% of IT projects fail because senior management doesn't get involved and the requirements scope change. So, for example, the project was rather small and then it got to a huge size, for example. And senior management doesn't react accordingly to some customer interactions in order to be in scope. And another one statistics for you: 78% of respondents feel that business is out of synchronization with project requirements.

And business stakeholders need to be more involved in the process. And when we define some specifics, or in other words, some requirements for the project. Then the team should follow these requirements in order to complete the desired project. And last but not the least, poor estimation during the planning phase continues to be the largest contributor to IT project failures with 72% of events. So the estimation and the planning phase, how hard this task is, how many team members do we need and so on. It is one of the weak points of project management for the current situation in the IT market. So, dear friends, that was a chapter dedicated to project management activities. See you in the following one.

Uncertainty in IT

Welcome back. And this chapter will be dedicated to such a high degree of uncertainty in I.T. projects. This term is from the probabilistic theory of some thing of open and closed information. And the IT industry is some kind of industry with such closed information which is hard to forecast. And this chart helps us to see which roles have major uncertainty. So we're starting from the biggest degree of uncertainty. Then the sales manager faced the biggest one. So they don't know many details that will be a successful project or know what. Will the team be capable of being OK with skills and so on.

But they believe that the company should accomplish the goal. And so the next role is project management. And they see more certainty in the project. They have some resources, some teams and some experience, and they are more confident in the certainty of completion of the project. The next line of business is the role of business analyst, and they try to diminish such uncertainty even further. By creating certification requirements, working with clients and the team and trying to be a bridge between their team of specialists and the customers.

And then software architects come into play in building architecture and the projects can be seen in some pictures and some technologies and some kind of tech solutions on the level of architecture. Software developers are bringing even more certainty into the practice as they are estimating the features' difficulties. And on what time frame the team can solve these issues. Then the quality assurance team comes into place. But the methodology is that they're trying to be in the project from the very beginning, from the business analysis, the and the making of some test cases and other quality assurance practices in order to make the formula nonfunctional, and the characteristics of the product suitable for marketing use them.

Technical writers come into place and they write in some kind of documentation where all unnecessary, even technical jargons are trying to be removed in order to write in simple language. Which is concise and not ambiguous for the end customers. And the uncertainty is at its lowest level. There are some practices in order to help these specialists to maintain the lowest possible level of uncertainty. So they are the following: It reduces uncertainty through detailed planning, some kind of project boundaries and requirements for their products. Setting "smart" goals. It is set for specific, measurable attainment, realistic, and time-bound goals.

And check compliance with business goals. IT goals should be aligned with business goals in order to satisfy them, as well as technical staff of customer and business lines. And check compliance with business goals and business goals should be in nice alignment as was mentioned. Each feature, ideally, should bring in some business value. Also making plans with customers. Oh, maybe not, but some kind of reliable partner where each stakeholder is interested in the project and should be involved and engaged in the project activities. And assembling a team that starts and implements and finishes the project in one lineup. So not many changes in the team and rather a stable team, which knows its velocity, its speed, or for resolving issues, will be a nice practice.

And having the professional manager of the product owner. So if the project manager has nice experience, it is not the very young, inexperienced one, but has some projects in his experience and knows how to maintain the scope, time, and budget. They, of course, could also be a nice product supporter also in the project. Alright, dear friends. Thank you for being with me in this chapter. Thank you for your attention. See you in the following one.

IT Projects

Dear friends, Welcome back. This chapter will be dedicated to such things as project management tools. When we talk about project management tools, the common ones are the following: It could be popular things like Excel, for example, or Microsoft Project, or getting help from consulting companies, or some kind of outsourcing management activities. And if we're focused on custom software development, then the whole tool comes into place. It is JIRA or Redmine, for example, and some support for Google Docs spreadsheets. If we're talking about Google's suite, it could be used. Also, Microsoft suits could be possible also with Excel, Outlook, Microsoft projects and Skype for business communication or Microsoft teams. Now they're popular tools in the business context for project management.

They are the common ones. For example, some examples of Microsoft projects or diagrams, data in some kind of gantt charts, shots with some schedule, for example, bring in some project management activities for analysts and with time frames other specifics for tasks. And if we're moving further them, comes into play some methodologies to use those more efficient And we are talking about major ones they are agile family with specific things as Scrum, Kanban, Lean. And another one is kind of like a waterfall and so on. So to two major families for project management, the classic one is waterfall and and the other one is agile practices and there are other methodologies as well. They are Six Sigma for introducing the biggest quality possible with 99.98% of quality.

If we're talking about some major requirements, the quality of the products and a reduction of bugs. And ASAP for SAP context as accelerated SAP. One of the classics of things in the IT industry is RUP methodology: stands for rational unified process. Some Britain methodology as prince two: project in controlled environments. And some definitions for you to solidify your knowledge of projects. It is successful: and the project was one that may have all three of the triple constraints. And these constraints are the following to meet the cost of the product, not to use more. And be in the scope of not implementing many features.

And a challenging project. That is a project which has met two of three constraints, for example, schedule and cost. But not all features were implemented for, for example, many unnecessary features. For whatever reason, they were implemented. Or, for example, where all the features were implemented well with the alright Book, but not in the time which was agreed. And you can continue to think about some kind of failed project. That is one that was canceled before it was completed or was not completed, or was completed, but not used at all. So there were some different challenges, some paradigm shifts or whatever.

But the results are not necessary for the time of completion and so on. Maybe some foresight at work. Some statistics now for you and project success rates in agile and waterfall methodologies. And if we are talking about agile methodologies roughly 40% of each project are successful. Half of them are challenged and nearly 10 percent of such projects fail. If we are talking about the classic waterfall, then the quarter of the projects are successful and the half is challenged and we have rather one in the fixed projects available. So the waterfall has some kind of big failure rate. And if we're talking about waterfalls, I can remind you or introduce that there is a brief stage of the waterfall later, we will find out more details from this methodology and others.

But for now, as an introduction, there are four stages on the high level of the waterfall. It is the requirements, what to build and what our system should accomplish. Then design some kind of architecture, bringing this architecture to the development team, which will create this project. And after it introduces some quality characteristics in order to try and find some bugs in the products. So there are some specifics in each methodology and of course, each product and tool which was mentioned about these things in the following chapters. Thank you for your attention. See you in the following chapter.

Intro to Agile and its Manifesto

Dear friends, welcome back after an introduction to some major tools of project management and some kind of project management methodologies and finding out the generic life-cycle of waterfall methodology we are starting to describe and to talk about the major families of methodologies in the information technology domain. And it is agile methodologies. And we will talk about them on a high level. Later, we will find out more of them. But now I'm introducing different kinds of agile methodologies. Agile methodologies start with so-called documents and it is the agile manifesto. They stated four major things for agile software development.

They are the following: Individuals and interaction over process and tools. And working product over comprehensive documentation. Customer collaboration over industry and responding to change over following the plan. some know it. That is well, there is value in the item on the right side of the table. They also show the document value, the artists on the left more. So they value individual interactions over some strict processes, organization and strict tools. So, for example, if a customer wants to talk, doesn't want to talk on Skype or Microsoft team and another tool could be introduced slack or another one.

Or, for example, a working product over a comprehensive documentation In some kinds of waterfall projects, there is some habit of making one hundred, two or three, and three hundred documents. And to describe the features, describe the specifics of the product. But at the end of the day, the product could not be working at all. And this happens in 1/5 or 20% of their events. So it is nice to have a working documentation lot there. And we just need to have a working product. The third is customer collaboration over contract negotiation. It is kind of trying to be not too formal, not too strict with contract negotiations, to work only inside the contract.

But it's a nice thing to have to be in the legal field. But to work more than only in the legal field, but to collaborate with customers, to engage with stakeholders, to be in a friendly atmosphere, to be in some kind of a big team with the customer. And the fourth one is responding to change over following a plan. And we see it usually done following a plan in waterfall methodologies. It is another thing which could lead to failure of the project because a project would be according to some plan and it could even be a construct in a good way. And so each category is okay, but the paradigm shifted and for example, the product would be disrupted at all.

For example, who from what industry or whatever organization faced some problems. And if they are working only inside the plan and are not responding to some changing market in a global economy, they could lead this product to failure. And we continue with such methodology as Scrum. We're talking about scrum methodology. This is kind of a tricky methodology, because it's rather simple, but it's hard to implement and should be adaptable to the situation and used in the right manner in order to be successful. So studying this methodology with this kind of vision and after the vision is set and the product backlog is constructed.

Backlog is a list of features to be concise and a list of features, but they are prioritized according to the desires of customers. And then there are events such as sprint planning meetings. In this meeting some scrum teams define and review product backlogs. So trying to prioritize them. Then they set up a sprint goal. And sprint is some kind of time frame for from one to four weeks. And in the sprint planning meeting, the team will define the goal of the sprint. And they sprint backlog. So how many features from the main backlog will be involved in the spring backlog, so some subset of the backlog will be implemented. They then commit to the sprint. So they bet ,the team that will do these features in this time frame.

And after that team sprint backlog aside to Sprint and it is estimated by a team. If we're talking about estimation, then it would be a different approach to this. One of the classic ones is such a thing as planning poker. When team members try to assign some kind of Fibonacci numbers, for example, for estimating how hard it will be to implement the feature. So to be concise and simple, one clear point, for example, is to rather warm-up activities for a warming-up feature, for example, 10 or another number for a very hard thing. But the number comes from Fibonacci's series. So not all numbers will apply in the classic one. And then there is the ritual in scrum, which is called daily scrum.

And then the team that's there during the sprint. It is also a rather short thing for 10, 15 minutes and it is some kind of stand-up activity and not anyone in the team sitting during these activities. If one is in a standing pose in order to be in active mode and they are trying to answer three questions. What has this team member done since the last meeting? And what plan does this member have for this day? And what obstacles could prevent him from making success? And then they are trying to work on the spring goals and trying to deliver on its goal commitments. Then the sprint review comes into place and review and activity which is dedicated to some demonstrations of features to customers.

So it is a collaborative effort of the team and customers in order to agree that features are delivered and they are doing OK. And this sprint was a success, for example, or not success and its interaction with customers about the features with some kind of real demonstration. And real demonstration should be on shippable product increment. And so, for example, a working feature, for example, a registration feature or login feature or another one. And after the demonstration or interview was completed to start in such activities as sprint retrospective, it is an internal activity, it is done inside the team without the customer.

Their team tries to agree on best practices for the activities, worst practices should be decreased in the process, the team members could try not to make it too personal by trying to diminish their best practices and to increase nice work practices during sprints. And then they repeat the cycle once again. Thank you for being with me on this chapter dedicated to scrum introduction and agile manifesto. In the following chapter, we will continue with such things as Kanban. And thank you for your attention. See you in the following chapter.

Agile: Kanban

Welcome back. After making some brief statements about your manifesto and one of the most popular agile methodologies such as Scrum, we are ready for another methodology of Agile. Kanban comes from the Japanese corporation Toyota and Kan stands for some kind of. card in and some 'Ban' for the signal from Japanese, is some kind of card which were first introduced in the card manufacturing industry. Car producer is from Japan, and it is Toyota. So it's some kind of card and one of the major artifacts in the campaign methodology is called the KanBan board. We see this board subprocesses with so- called pools. And starting from the left of these boards is reviewed. And the first thing is such a backlog queue. We understand that backlog is some kind of list of features and we know it from scrumpy introductions.

And so they can see some kinds of features in their backlog. They are prioritized for meeting the most desired ones on the customer for this period of time. And then some cards came to the phone late. And for example, it is our current top priority queue. So the most urgent thing to do and after it the team sees that there, for example, are four things in this column and they are starting to work on something on some feature, then come into place, into the progress column, after it. When this feature is ready to be shippable in the opinion of all developers, for example, they complete the registration feature with social media buttons. They are moving this card to the column, which is called to be verified and verified.

it is genetic to be verified, but it could be verified by a business analyst or designer or in the classics and it could be verified by quality assurance. And so, for example, if the quality assurance schemes make this statement that it is OK, then the feature could be done and implemented into production environments and for example, to be looking for registration with social media and there are some tricks to these kanban boards. So the major thing for introduction, it will be understanding that it is not good to have many features in progress. Or, for example, only one. So it's kind of medium activity should be implemented, there are no sprints in classic KanBan So no time frames are builded to some kind of feature. No two-four weeks to four weeks period. But we are trying to finish work in progress.

Rational Unified Process - RUP

Dear friends, welcome back. This chapter will be dedicated to some introduction of classic methodology in order to solidify your understanding of the IT industry, the moment not only agile methodology, but a classic one. And this one is a rational unified process or RUP for short. The RUP methodology is an iterative software development process. And if we are talking about iterations, the major concept of this iteration. So kind of a repeatable cycle. So for making some cyclic actions of initiation, executing and so on and one cycle, then the second one and the third one and so on, Repeating an increase in quality, for example, and making more in this cycle.

And so it is an iterative software development process from IBM and it is a framework which is created by a rational software corporation. And it is some kind of subdivision of IBM. And it was invented in 2003. And is not a concrete prescriptive process, but it's a rather adaptable process and framework. And scrum it's another kind of framework, for example. This framework is intended in cases such as RUP to be tailored by the development organization and software project teams that will select the elements of the process that are appropriate for the needs of the customers. RUP a specific implementation of the Unified Process.

So in fact, this is some kind of overall term and a unified process, a kind of subdivision of these unified approaches and some kind of IBM creation. RUP is based on set building blocks and content elements, which describes what should be produced and the necessary skills of the team which are required and step by step explanation describing how specific development goals are to be achieved. The main building blocks and content elements are the following: So the major thing is roles (who?). A role defines a set of related skills related to this role, some competencies and responsibilities for these humans who will perform this role. And what products are sold.

The question "what?" our product representatives, something which results from a task including all the documents and models, which should be produced while working through the process. And "tasks", "How?" and tasks describe a unit, the work which is assigned to a role that provides a meaningful result for the business. All right. We find some additional information on rational unified approaches. Within each iteration, the tasks are accurately characterized into nine disciplines. There are six engineering disciplines that are in this set.

They are the following: a business model in our requirements gathering, creating and developing analysis and design of the system, implementation of such a technology system, its testing and quality assurance and deployment to the end customer or for the client. And three supporting disciplines. Its configuration and change management tool to manage the change and scope of the project, project management activities and environment of such projects. So dear friends. This chapter was regarded as a rational unified process of IBM. Thank you for your attention. See you in the following chapters.

Activities and Services of IT Companies

Welcome back. After discovering such a methodology as Scrum and lean, some kanban practices were ready to be more specific to the activities of IT companies. They include some services and other things. The list is rather big but we mention the major one source, such as a provision of services for implementation of support or some business practices. processing data, some kind of database activities. depending on cryptographic information for security, audit or information system and software consultant. And we know of some major clients in this thing as Ernst and Young, for example.

Now some kind of start via EPAM technologies in the kind of I.T. consultant and for older kids and some young is an example and other big players. Social activities could be software release and promotion. Could be the gaming industry, as if we're talking marketing. It could be digital advertising and media services on the Internet used to develop software toolkits for search engine optimization for programmatic advertising. Also, IT services could also implement, develop and maintain software using transactions, blockchain registry technology or we know what kind of trends of blockchain.

and mining services for the creation placement or digital signs or activities of the exchange, crypto currencies or some kind of a in something on top of blockchain. If you want to know more blockchain and other financial systems, you can find it in chapter some additional links. Mining services for the creation of such things are included. Blockchain and bitcoin topics. Data services could be implemented by companies, for example, hosting websites and so on. Creating and training neural networks and other activities of artificial intelligence and also find some references in the end of the Book. And this is an area, for example, for artificial intelligence, with subdomains as machine learning and other things. Development and then the concept of Internet things.

Now we're talking about the domain of big data technologies. Technology developed for the financial sector is implemented rather than usual in its sectors and it as a core is also involved in such kinds of activities. One of the major trends in the IT industry is outsourcing, but with some specific for the IT industry. As a general outsourcing is a business practice in which a company has and as a company or an individual to perform tasks and handle operations or provide services that are either executed or had previously been done by the company's own employees. And there are processes of outsourcing, They are preinstalled from routine or non core tasks; also customer concentration on business goals and objectives could be attained.

There are some cost savings on such practices, but there are some minuses out of outsourcing. They are: out of good designers, and some develop critical services without proper guidance from the management. But they are so low and manageable. And of course this requires a nice reputation as an outsourcer. And if it is nice then that project will be OK for some instances. of course it is. If it is not a well equipped company, then the project would be available. But sometimes also management and the decision to make this project outsourced or not. It also should be considered in order to find the major pros, but not all of outsourcing.

And some examples, for example, of HTP: high tech residents of Belarus, for instance, for solidifying experience of probable ways to implement software companies. The majority of them are outsourcing services, but they are trying to customize technology solutions for tailoring the needs of clients and companies and trying to build customized products, development, support products for internal needs, for data centers, for example, and development centers, and to develop and support proprietary products, not open source. Also, they customize industry solutions or tailoring more needs in digital transformation.

Some advisory services, provision of for internal needs of the parent company and shared services centers, some research and development, scientific research, game development. E.g. we know, a collaboration of EPAM with epic games, for example, and other things. Educational services, outsourcing of business processes, customer hardware development and the implementation of IT infrastructure data centers and computers machinery and networks. And a further increase in your knowledge on types of IT outsourcing, not on a generic level, but on some specifics. It could be such a category as out staffing and dedicated teams.

If we talk about our staffing tasks, providing such kinds of employees to perform them. And the customer knows by name all members of its team. And also responsibility there are risks management downtime, loading light and telling the customer situation. And the company provided an office and the team was comfortable with working conditions, accounting, etc. If it needs some out of the staff team. If we're talking about a dedicated team, the team is the carrier of all technologies, architecture, development, experience and knowledge of the project. In such situations, the team only works full time on the customer's project and interacts with them directly, So this team could not perform many projects at a time. But they work solely on the project of the client in such a situation.

The customer is ready to invest in regular and continuous development. It's kind of more costly because it's required from an outsourced company dedicated team, which is assigned to only one product with some kind of long term growth and gradual development of such things. The customer then pays for the main work and the company takes over the management and control of the risk, but can share them with customers. And of course, this kind of agreement from the customer client in which percentage risks and values will be quite different. Dear friends, thank you for your attention in this chapter and see you in the following one.

Models of IT Outsourcing Services

Dear friends, welcome back, and after covering some specific IT activities with examples and some major partnerships and some kind of outsourcing model of collaboration and increasing it to dedicated teams and so on. We're ready to increase our knowledge in your understanding of the models of collaboration in the IT industry and introducing a fixed price model and time and material model. So if we're talking about a fixed pricing model and project implementation is done in accordance with that assessment. This assessment involves fixing the budget on some consistent value and time frame as a constant also. And then after this agreement, the outsource company could not make changes or additions after signing a contract.

And the client also. So they have the lock symbol as a metaphor and they are working on their thing, how they agreed on it. Another, more adaptable approach to outsourcing. It is time and material. Performing a task in time report, for example, schedule and distribution of resources between projects. And. And project activities could be implemented. Distribution of resources of some changes in the team task. Complexity and timing are possible and broken in both to the customer at the end or the iteration or cycle is implemented.

And there are of course some nice features of a fixed price model. Time and material and dedicated team and dedicated team was mentioned in the previous chapter. And now in order to be more specific, there are some categories on which these collaboration methodologies could be performed. They are the following. It is the size of the project, time frame and project flexibility. Clients have control over the process and development methodology and requirements. And if we are talking about a dedicated team from the previous chapter. It is nice to have our large projects which require such a dedicated team. And a time frame and budget are flexible and the client has full control over its dedicated team.

And it is the major force in this kind of interaction. And development methodology will be or agile or waterfall If we're talking about the big rather not needed In adaptation projects and requirements are evolving if we are talking about agile Mostly. And if we're talking about fixed price collaboration, which is introduced for you in this chapter, then the projects are usually small and medium where they can fix and predict the precise number of required resources. Because if it is large, it is rather difficult to predict the right measure and time frame is fixed. So they are fixed in time.

And this is great for small things because it could be predicted. Well, the time required to do a small project and client has little control over this process. And so usually it signed an agreement and that's all. It is upon the performance of the team to implement it. The development methodology is OK for basic waterfall and if it is a small project there it could be performed well with waterfall methodology and requirements are defined and strict and fixed. So the project will be implemented no matter what is going on in a strict manner. As it was signed. of course, in the lengthy project on big projects, it could lead to some failures at small scale.

It is ok practice. And time and material collaboration activity. And then it fits nicely to the medium of projects. Also, the time frame and project, as was mentioned, is flexible from both sides. Clients have significant but not full control over this process. Development methodologies, usually some kind of one of the agile family. It could be scrum. It could be kanban. It could be a combination of scrum and kanban so-called scrum ban. Also, the requirements are changing via agreements for cooperation between clients and the vendor of technology.

And to conclude If we have a fixed price, the companies agreed resources to be fixed. And if we are talking about time and material, they rather will be changing. And if we are talking about a dedicated team which is kind of one team which is signed to one customer, which will implement its activities. Dear friends That's it for this chapter. Thank you for your dedication to the topic of the software development industry and see you in the following one.

Types of IT Projects Funding

Dear friends, welcome back. After understanding collaboration of possible agreements on customers, it could be a fixed price, it could be time and scope or the negotiating team, for example. We are ready to find out some kind of funding for IT projects. So the major budget category and solidifying your understanding of financing of IT projects. And to solidify your notion, we should mention and remind you that the main goal of any business is not to figure out how to solve the problem. Don't make a lot of sales, don't find a cool designer who will do nicely. The main goal is to make money at the end of the day. It could also be used as a possible kind of funds of the own funds of business owners. It could be profit or some kind of resource of cash or savings. And it could use attractive funds.

It could be family, friends and fools and some kind of joint from startup context, investing borrowed money, funds or individuals for business angels. It could be a bank loan for a nice project is a good business plan. Crowdfunding - we know a crowdsourcing model. They are developing many projects and some kind of P2P lending, accelerator or incubator money could be used, some competition could be won. And state loans are also a possible solution for some goals. And also on the lowest level business angels could help I.T. companies to solidify its startups. On the more senior stages venture capital Investment could be involved if they see possible rapid growth of IT-startup.

And other stages in the life cycle of enterprise were entrepreneurs and moves from the idea stage to securing financing, laying down the basic structure of the business and initiating operation or trading. And in order you to do some startup things and possible startup problems could be faced. Also, the complexity of prioritizing features of the new enterprise and product development management. Slow development.

If this is a problem we should discuss such solutions as using the backend approach as a service, For solving slow development. If we are talking about prioritizing features or some kind of design in a broad sense, we prioritize the major features, which could help to solve these problems.

And one of the other problems of an IT start-up is little attention to user experience and user interfaces. Now we will introduce you, for example, popular technologies which are implemented by High Tech Park in order for you to understand the major trending ICT systems and information systems, The major fields of IT is: This Internet of Things, then comes into play, Artificial intelligence, machine learning, some gamification procedures in ~19 percent of situations. AI expert systems and chatbots. We shall also stand on artificial intelligence and machine learning. Some kinds of drones are introduced into such pandemic and post-pandemic contexts.

Where services are of a high degree of importance and new vehicles are introduced and drones If the requirements with government bodies are fulfilled and nice startups which are viable and block chain startups are also increasing needs. Market shares in the kind of proof certificates from government bodies, from banking services and so on. Artificial intelligence is also in place with each of them in the machine known as was mentioned. But also augmented reality and virtual reality are also nice trends in I.T. industry. Also, some part of artificial development as NLP in this context is not neuro linguistic programming from psychology but natural language processing. Some kind of recognition of human speech, 3D printing is also good with introducing 3D printers. Some I.T.

projects are 3D printed. Autonomous vehicles are also increasing not only for drones for flying machines with machine learning technologies, but for trucks and other things. And RPA as robotic process automation, but not robots from sci-fi films with hands and legs, but some kind of software program, which could implement some roles activities, for example, some business clerks and so on. Dear friends this was a chapter dedicated to the types of funding I.T. projects, particularly I.T. startups.

It could be its own money and the angels of the business to make money for start-up to evolve and to bring some value for its investors from early stage business angels and for later stages - venture capitalists. And startups could be in different areas of possible I.T. trends as artificial intelligence, RPA If you want to learn more about these topics, find info in bonus chapter, some references. And for now, that's it for it-startup, it's types of fundings and possible financing of IT. Thank you for being with me in this chapter. See you in the following one.

IT Projects' Roles I

Dear friends, welcome back. We talked about software development teams on the high level, which roles will be involved in software products as usual. Now let's focus on more details on some of the roles. And let's start with the following thing. We will discuss some project management activities, some business analysis and so on. So starting with the project manager and project manager by definition is a specialist responsible for the successful implementation of the project: in time specified by customer, as we remember, with a necessary quality, with a fixed budget, limited human resources, and in accordance with the requirements of the customer.

So many constraints should be performed by the project manager. And what other activities of the project manager: to be to the left of the customer. And it does not go into the details of the requirements. It offers solutions, effectively communicates, and solves problems of the project. Handle tasks and plans of this project. It relentlessly delegates issues for best performance and reports to the customer what is going on and what skills do project management should have. It is: hard skills, soft skills, conversational English. If we are talking about how skilled: at some kind of understanding of the high-level programming knowledge, it is databases, but not in specific detail, but at a high level, what time is needed for implementation of some detail.

Some soft skills to talk with employees, with team members, to be in good shape to perform best. Project management methodologies: we discussed some of this agile and agile family and team player motivators. So that is the project manager. And if we are talking about a software architect, it is the role which makes conceptual decisions about how the system will be built, what kind of technology will be used, what framework of programming languages. For example, javascript could be used for front-end activities, but its frameworks could be used, NodeJS, for example, for backend activities and from the requirements architect, it receives information about visibility, speed, or labor intensity for such a project.

If we are talking about software engineers or software developers, this role implements the requirements which are described by the business analyst. And in practice, software developers often look more at the title, the justification, and read the text only fluently. It is not a good thing because it could lead to bugs, but it is some kind of reality. Software developers could be asking business analysts very specific questions if they need some attention required for implementing detail. And of course, it is nice to have conversations with software developers and business analysts about the superior quality and nice quality of the products. And now comes into place benefits from high quality business analysis.

And this comes from some kind of interaction between business analysts with clients and with software developments. These practices could lead to nice results: such as fewer defects in requirements, in the finished product. Fewer reworks. Rework requires money and it could lead to project failure. Faster development and delivery of the finished product. Fewer unnecessary and unused features.

So only the necessary features should be implemented, not very many. The number should be optimal, not the maximum. Lower the cost of the modification. Less misunderstanding, fewer project boundaries, less clutter or waste, as was mentioned in lean methodology. Higher customer satisfaction and products that do not need what is not expected from them, but do what is expected from these projects. Dear friends, thank you for being with me on this theme and covering some roles in more detail. See you in the following chapters.

IT Projects' Roles II

Dear friends, welcome back. And now this chapter will be dedicated to further discovering the rules of IT teams and in the previous chapter, we mention such roles as system architect, business analyst, some kind of its practices, and project manager. Now we are ready for the following one. And we're starting with a quality assurance engineer or software tester. And it is on different terms because the tester regards the current system and it is not working in advance and quality assurance it is working in advance and trying to find the things before it comes to production.

And a tester from definition, to solidify your knowledge, is the person who identifies bugs in its work and corrects them. But this product should be in production. So it is not working in advance as was mentioned. A more agile way is to work with quality assurance engineers who are trying to find defects starting from requirements, phase and so on. And now talking about testers. This person checks the requirements for completeness, consistency and quality of description and quality assurance. It's more relevant. This role checks artifacts for compliance with agreements adopted in the draft. It is based on the approved requirements and develops test cases. Its role controls the quality of the software being developed.

So regarding the control phase project. We are seeing some possible artifacts or software testers and this role writes test cases. Test cases are a kind of artifact and one of the major tools for using these is basic excel. But it could be used with more sophisticated tools from open source: e.g. RedMine, to some commercial systems such as JIRA and so on. And it could be the following columns for these documents. As "ID", "name" of the test case, some of the steps which should be implemented to perform. Some expected result and actual results of such kind of activity. And now let's switch to such roles as user interface and user experience designer. And the interface is always an interaction of system, human or user interaction.

And UI is a user interface. And UX is user experience. User experience includes a variety of complex information architecture and interaction design, graphic design and content. And user experience design is a comprehensive approach to user interaction with the interface. Whether, its website or mobile app, or some other type of program, or on another device. The task of a UI specialist is to develop interfaces as possible to take into account all the necessary details from the environment and the type of digital device to the ways in which information is displayed to the user in the most convenient way. So switching to such a role as technical writer.

This role is based on the requirement described by the business analyst. Technical writers preparing manuals and instructions, helps to make the system more convenient. So some work with internal documents and preparing the documents for clients and customers and then users: some manuals on how to use and to be more described without being unambiguous in clear, plain English. Or in context of the language of target application. So technically, that was a technical writer. Dear friends, thank you for being part of the introduction to the roles of a software team. See you in the following one.

SDLC models: Cascade, Iterative, Spiral

Dear friends, welcome to this chapter dedicated to the system development life cycle. After understanding the roles on the high level and some details of these roles activities we are ready for understanding such system analysts concepts as part of the software development lifecycle. Not only project management, but with some specifics of technologies. And software lifecycle, but now generic one. The software life cycle model is a period of time that begins when a software product is decided to be created and ends when it is completely decommissioned and from ending the cycle to its end. And SDLC models could be of different types.

It is kind of a coding error fixing models and tasks performing and checking the results and generic one some cascade models. The models are developed through testing and some of "V" models with the emphasis on software testing practices. A prototype-based model, spiral model and flexible model. These models and some will be introduced to you right now in this chapter in order to solidify your knowledge in classics of software development practices and some solid, fundamental things. All right. We're moving forward. And we start with a cascade model.

There are the following stages in this model. It is a requirement analysis, design, development, testing, maintenance phase. So we start up from some kind of waterfall model with generic steps. We will now implement more sophisticated details for things in this particular example on the cascade model. So from analysis of requirements by business analysts and quality assurance engineers, designing the system, creating it and maintaining this system. There are some disadvantages of this model. And there could be no feedback between the implemented stages.

And it doesn't meet the real conditions for software development goals: requirements are changing, the situation, the market are rather flexible and so on. But there are some advantages: consistently run the project stages in a fixed order. No chaos in this model. It's rather ordered and it is a nice thing. And it allows us to evaluate the project team because there is a product at each stage. For each product, there are some quality checks if it is OK and then moving on. So moving forward. Also there are such models as spiral models. There is some cycling in this and it is planning the determining objectives, planning the tests and development plan and planning requirements. And this model is doing with a high degree of interaction with project risks. And this model tries the results, the risks.

So there is a risk analysis, a number of prototypes to find out these risks. And then after identifying risk, the activities move to development and testing. So some kind of requirements, drafts, detailed design by designers are available. Some code is written and integration takes place and test implementation and then planning the next iteration. So making this spiral once again and reusing some activities for one cycle to another one. And now the next model for you is a flexible model. Or an iterative model. There are some good things, there are advantages, and it's reducing risks because it minimizes the cost of eliminating them. And effective feedback from the projects with users.

So this kind of model introduces focus on the most important critical task by identifying risks, and we continue from the previous chapter. And it is a continuum of interactive testing, one iteration, second and so on. Early detection of conflicts between requirements, models and project implementations. More loading of project participants with the necessary artifacts. Effective use of experience from stage, from previous stages. And real assessment of the current state of the project. So flexible and spiral model details are introduced and they are nice to have. And now we are ready to recap on this chapter.

So there are some quizzes we will discuss together. And let's start with such a question. Where can programmers find full information about specific programming language, module or framework technology. It could be Facebook.com, documentation, source code or at StackOverflow . And if we are talking about stack-overflow, it is, of course, popular and the majority of the time, the programmers are trying to find a solution to help each other. In source code they have some details, but it needs documentation of programming languages as the major source of some specification of programming language model framework technologies. Right. Let's move to the next question.

And if we are talking about the next question, let's mention something like What is a "Stack Overflow" web-portal? A: A portal devoted to algorithms and computer science. B: The largest question and answer site for programmers. C: A bug that happens when a program tries to write to the memory address. D: A method that defines a specific search pattern. So starting from option A. It is not the particular portal devoted to algorithms and computer science, but it is the largest question and answer site for programmers, where some programmers will post questions and some of them can answer them. But it's not the bug and not the method that defines a specific search pattern. And question number three, who is generally responsible for conducting business analysis activity in an organization.

Whether it is A: quality assurance engineer or B: DevOps engineer or C: designer or D: business analyst. And it is not the quality assurance specialist who is conducting business analysis, not DevOps, which is trying to make some automation of the process to the customer. It is not the designer, which brings some activities in Photoshop and other Adobe, for example, software tools, but it is a business analyst. So option D is correct. And moving forward to question number four. Waterfall software development is one of the types of agile methodology. Whether it is true or false. And we know that there are a bunch of agile frameworks and some classic methodologies.

But waterfall it's not a subset of agile. So this statement is false. Alright dear friends. You can remember and enhance your understanding of such questions in the interactive exercises, and find additional questions for you to solve. For now great dedication from your side. Well done. See you soon in the following chapters. 28. From Garage Innovators to Global Giants: Tracing the Dynamic Evolution of the IT

Welcome to "From Garage Innovators to Global Giants: The Evolution of the Software Industry". In this paper, we embark on a journey through time to explore the remarkable evolution of the software development industry. From its humble beginnings in the 1950s, when computers transitioned from academic labs to business environments, to its present-day status as a cornerstone of the digital economy, we delve deep into the growth, trends, and future prospects of this dynamic mega-industry. The software industry, once composed of niche technical tools, has transformed rapidly, catalyzing profound changes in how we live, work, and communicate.

Through the pages of this paper, we aim to shed light on the origins of this industry, trace its exponential growth, and unravel the key factors that have shaped its current landscape. By examining the business models, technological advancements, and remarkable success stories of both pioneering startups and established tech giants, we will provide concrete examples and valuable insights into the software industry's trajectory. Additionally, we will explore the evolving workforce dynamics, changing skill requirements, and emerging trends that are shaping the industry's future.

Through robust research, industry analysis, and thought-provoking observations, we aim to equip readers with a comprehensive understanding of the software development industry's past, present, and future. Whether you are an industry professional, a technology enthusiast, or simply curious about the inner workings of one of the most influential industries of our time, this paper will serve as your guide into the captivating world of software. Join us as we unfold the chronicles of the software industry, exploring the remarkable journey from garage innovators to global giants. Let us embark on this enlightening exploration together and gain invaluable insights into the power, growth, and future potential of this transformative industry.

The Mainframe Era: 1950s-1970s

The software industry's nascent years, spanning from the 1950s to the 1970s, marked the dawn of the mainframe era. During this period, key players such as IBM and CSC emerged as pioneers, concentrating on mainframe computers and developing custom applications and system software primarily for government agencies and large organizations. In the mainframe-dominated market, revenue models predominantly revolved around long-term licenses and maintenance fees. Unlike the consumer-driven software landscape we see today, the mainframe software market centered on creating reliable, large-scale solutions tailored for institutional clients rather than individual consumers.

This created a highly profitable environment known as the "glass house" culture, where organizations relied on mainframes and the associated software to support their critical operations. Examples of noteworthy software companies that thrived during this era include IBM, which introduced the IBM System/360 mainframe series in 1964, revolutionizing the industry with its compatibility across various models. IBM's dominance and commitment to quality software set the stage for its continued success and influence in subsequent decades. Control Data Corporation (CDC) is another exemplary company that contributed to the mainframe era. CDC developed the CDC 6600, one of the earliest supercomputers introduced in the 1960s.

This powerful mainframe's software capabilities enabled scientific and engineering breakthroughs, serving as a catalyst for advancements in diverse fields. During the mainframe era, software companies faced limited competition, allowing them to establish robust market positions and generate substantial profits. The mainframe market's emphasis on serving institutional clients further bolstered this profit-generating culture. Key insights from the mainframe era include:

The dominance of mainframe computers and the software developed for them laid the foundation for the software industry's future growth and innovation. Long-term licenses and maintenance fees became the primary revenue models during this era.

The mainframe era primarily catered to institutional clients, emphasizing reliable and scalable solutions over consumer-oriented software. Established companies like IBM and CDC played pivotal roles in advancing mainframe technology and creating a highly profitable market environment. The mainframe era laid the groundwork for subsequent periods in the software industry's evolution, setting the stage for dramatic changes and advancements that would follow. Let us now delve further into the next phase, where the industry witnessed the emergence of personal computers and the birth of software entrepreneurship.

The PC Software Evolution: 1980s-1990s

The advent of personal computers in the 1980s and 1990s marked a significant shift in the software industry, opening it up to retail consumers and small businesses [1]. This era witnessed the rise of various software segments, each with its own unique contributions and revenue drivers. One notable example during this period is Microsoft Office, a suite of productivity tools that became a major revenue driver for the software industry. Microsoft Office, which included applications like Word, Excel, and PowerPoint, revolutionized the way individuals and businesses managed their documents, spreadsheets, and presentations.

Its success showcased the potential of software to enhance productivity and efficiency in both personal and professional settings. Moreover, the PC software evolution saw the emergence of new software segments catering to different needs. Operating systems like Microsoft Windows (as evolution of Microsoft's MS-DOS) became crucial components of the PC ecosystem, providing a user-friendly interface and enabling software compatibility across a wide range of hardware configurations. Desktop publishing software, such as Adobe PageMaker and QuarkXPress, empowered individuals and small businesses to create professional-looking publications, transforming the publishing industry.

Graphics software, like Adobe Photoshop, revolutionized image editing and manipulation, enabling creative professionals to push the boundaries of visual design. The gaming industry also experienced significant growth during this period, with popular titles like Doom and SimCity captivating a growing audience of PC gamers. Educational software also gained traction, with programs like The Oregon Trail and Reader Rabbit providing interactive learning experiences for kids. The shift from custom development to packaged software brought about affordable standardization.

Shrinkwrapped off-the-shelf software became widely available, allowing consumers and businesses to access a variety of applications at a lower cost. This shift prompted software firms to invest heavily in developing new features, exploring different licensing models, and expanding distribution channels to reach a broader market. Insights from the PC software evolution era: The PC boom enabled software to reach retail consumers and small businesses, significantly expanding the market.

Productivity tools like Microsoft Office became major revenue drivers due to their widespread adoption and usefulness in various work environments. Various software segments emerged, including operating systems, desktop publishing, graphics, games, and educational software, broadening the industry's scope. Shrink-wrapped, off-the-shelf software brought affordability and standardization, fueling competition and innovation.

Client-Server and The Internet Age: 1990s-2000s

The 1990s to the 2000s marked a significant period in the software industry with the emergence of client-server computing and the widespread adoption of the Internet. These advancements created a surge in demand for network infrastructure software and web-based applications, transforming various industries and driving technological innovation. During this era, the software industry experienced exponential growth as software applications began to permeate every aspect of business and daily life. The slogan "software ate the world" became a common phrase to highlight how software solutions became integral to the functioning of diverse sectors, including banking, retail, telecommunications, healthcare, and more.

Enterprise resource planning (ERP) systems, such as SAP, gained prominence during this time. These systems facilitated business process automation by integrating various departments and functions within organizations. ERP solutions provided a centralized platform for managing operations, including finance, human resources, supply chain, and customer relationship management. The rise of client-server architecture and the Internet also led to the development of horizontal middleware.

Middleware software acted as a bridge between different applications and systems, enabling seamless integration and data exchange. This allowed businesses to leverage existing software investments while adding new capabilities and functionalities. Additionally, the client-server and Internet age witnessed a significant increase in offshoring and software services. Many companies sought cost-effective labor by outsourcing software development, maintenance, and support to countries with lower labor costs. Offshoring allowed businesses to tap into a global talent pool and achieve cost efficiencies while meeting the growing demand for software solutions.

Insights from the Client-Server and The Internet Age: The expansion of client-server computing and the Internet drove the demand for network infrastructure software and web-based applications. Software development accelerated across sectors like banking, retail, telecom, healthcare, and more, as software became a prominent part of business operations. Enterprise resource planning (ERP) systems like SAP disrupts (in a positive manner) business process automation and resource management. Horizontal middleware played a vital role in integrating and connecting diverse software systems.

SaaS, Mobile Computing, and The Cloud: 2000s-Present

The 2000s to the present era witnessed significant advancements in the software industry with the rise of Software as a Service (SaaS), mobile computing, and the cloud [3]. These technological shifts have transformed the way software is delivered, enabling interconnected ecosystems and fueling innovation. SaaS, or cloud-based software delivery, has revolutionized the industry by providing on-demand access to software applications through the internet. Platforms like Salesforce, Amazon Web Services (AWS), and Microsoft Azure have emerged as leaders in creating interconnected ecosystems, where users can seamlessly integrate various software services and leverage cloud infrastructure for scalability and flexibility.

The hyper-scale cloud infrastructure offered by providers like AWS and Azure has enabled real-time, distributed computing, opening doors for complex and data-intensive applications. This infrastructure has also fueled the growth of "as-a-service" models, such as Platform as a Service (PaaS) and Infrastructure as a Service (IaaS), allowing businesses to shift their entire IT infrastructure to the cloud, reducing costs and improving operational efficiency. Open-source software has played a crucial role in this era, providing reusable components and benefiting collaboration and interoperability.

Open-source projects like Linux, Apache, and MySQL have become the foundation for many software applications and have fostered a culture of community-driven development and innovation. Furthermore, the infusion of Artificial Intelligence (AI) and Machine Learning (ML) has automated software capabilities and opened new horizons for intelligent applications. AI-powered solutions are being integrated into various software domains, ranging from customer service chatbots to advanced analytics and predictive modeling. Looking ahead, emerging technologies like serverless computing, edge computing, and quantum computing hold the potential to drive the next paradigm shifts in the software industry.

Serverless architectures allow developers to focus on writing code without worrying about infrastructure management, while edge computing brings processing power closer to the source of data, enabling real-time and low-latency applications. Quantum computing, still in its nascent stages, promises to revolutionize computing by solving complex problems exponentially faster than traditional computers. Insights from the SaaS, Mobile Computing, and The Cloud era: SaaS and mobile computing shifted software delivery to the cloud, enabling on-demand access and reducing the need for local installation.

Cloud platforms like AWS and Azure facilitated real-time, distributed computing and fueled the growth of "as-a-service" models. Open-source development paved the way for collaboration, reuse, and interoperability among software components. AI and ML technologies have infused software with automation, personalization, and smarter decision-making capabilities.

Key Trends Shaping the IT Industry

The software industry continues to evolve, with several key trends shaping its trajectory. These trends reflect the changing needs and demands of both businesses and consumers. Let's explore some of these trends: Expanding variety: Software now controls more aspects of our lives than ever before. From smart home devices and wearable technology to automotive systems and healthcare applications, software has become deeply integrated into various industries, enhancing functionality and improving user experiences. Time-to-market over perfectionism: In today's fast-paced digital landscape, organizations prioritize getting their software to market quickly.

Agile development methodologies have gained popularity, emphasizing iterative releases and continuous improvement, allowing companies to respond to market needs and customer feedback in a timely manner. Subscription and consumption-based business models: Traditional software licensing models are being replaced by subscription and consumption-based models. This enables users to pay for software as a service, providing flexibility and scalability while reducing upfront costs. This shift has led to the rise of Software as a Service (SaaS) providers, offering cloud-based solutions accessible on-demand.

Demands for greater security, privacy, and ethics: With the increasing prevalence of data breaches and privacy concerns, there is a growing demand for software that prioritizes security and privacy. Users expect their personal data to be protected, and organizations must adhere to ethical practices when developing and deploying software solutions. Platform consolidation and API ecosystems: As the software landscape becomes more complex, there is a trend towards platform consolidation and the development of API ecosystems.

Companies are integrating their software into platforms that offer various services, allowing for seamless integration and interoperability between different applications. Remote and asynchronous distributed teamwork: The COVID-19 pandemic (and post-pandemic period) has accelerated the adoption of remote work practices. Distributed teams collaborate across different time zones, relying on communication and collaboration tools to work effectively. Asynchronous work models are becoming more prevalent, enabling teams to operate across different schedules and locations. Automating coding via AI and low-code tools: Artificial Intelligence (AI) and low-code development platforms are transforming the software development process.

AI is being used to automate coding tasks, improve code quality, and assist developers in debugging and optimization. Low-code platforms allow developers to create applications with minimal hand-coding, enabling faster development cycles and empowering citizen developers. These trends reflect the direction in which the software industry is heading, driven by the need for efficiency, flexibility, and user-centric solutions. Conclusion Throughout the span of over 70 years, the software industry has undergone remarkable advancements, evolving from specialized systems to becoming an essential digital substrate that underpins innovation, productivity, and connectivity on a global scale.

The continuous progress of software has brought forth revolutionary capabilities, further ingraining itself into the fabric of society. As software continues to permeate every aspect of our lives, the industry now carries significant responsibilities in ensuring security, privacy, and ethical computing practices. With its profound influence, it is crucial for software developers and organizations to prioritize the protection of user data, respect privacy rights, and uphold ethical standards. When implemented thoughtfully and ethically, software has the power to uplift lives and drive progress for humanity. It enables us to solve complex problems, connect people across the globe, and enhance efficiency in various sectors. By harnessing the potential of software, we can create a positive impact and contribute to a better future.

As we move forward, it is vital for the software industry to continue fostering innovation, embracing emerging technologies, and addressing the challenges that come with its influence. By doing so, we can harness the full potential of software and leverage its capabilities to drive positive change and improve the lives of individuals and communities worldwide. Questions and Answers Q: How has software development methodologies changed over time? A: Software development methodologies have indeed evolved significantly over time to adapt to the changing needs of the industry. Initially, the waterfall methodology was widely used, which followed a sequential and linear process with distinct phases like requirements gathering, design, coding, and testing.

However, this approach had limitations in terms of flexibility and adapting to changing requirements. With the realization of the need for more iterative and collaborative approaches, methodologies like iterative development and agile emerged. Iterative development divided the development process into multiple cycles, allowing for feedback and adjustments along the way. Agile methodologies, such as Scrum and Kanban, further emphasized collaboration, frequent communication, and quick iterations to deliver incremental value to customers. The DevOps movement brought a significant shift by integrating development and IT operations, bridging the gap between development and deployment.

This approach focused on streamlining workflows, automation, and continuous integration and delivery, enabling faster and more efficient software development. Design thinking, influenced by human-centered design, brought empathy and user-centricity to software development. It emphasized prototyping, user testing, and rapid iteration to create solutions that truly meet user needs. Lean methodology, inspired by lean manufacturing principles, aimed to eliminate waste and optimize flow. This approach emphasized continuous improvement and encouraged rapid experimentation to drive efficiency and value. Overall, software development methodologies have shifted from rigid sequential processes to more flexible, adaptive, and collaborative approaches.

This evolution enables teams to respond quickly to customer feedback, embrace changing requirements, and deliver high-quality software in a timely manner. Q: What impact has open source software had on the industry? A: Open source software has had a profound impact on the software industry, influencing both technology and business models in various ways. One of the significant benefits of open source software is accelerated innovation. By allowing collaborative development and sharing of code, open source projects can rapidly evolve through contributions from a global community of developers. This fosters a culture of knowledge exchange and collaborative problem-solving, speeding up the development of new features and technologies.

Open source software also brings cost advantages by reducing duplicative efforts. Instead of reinventing the wheel, developers can leverage existing open source solutions, saving time and resources. This promotes efficiency and cost-effectiveness in software development. Furthermore, open source software promotes transparency and code review, enhancing security. Since the source code is publicly available, it can be audited by a large community, helping to identify and address vulnerabilities more effectively. This collective effort improves the overall security of the software. Interoperability is another significant advantage of open source software.

It enables seamless integration between different tools and platforms, fostering compatibility and reducing vendor lock-in. Open standards and open APIs allow for greater flexibility and choice in building software solutions. Open source software has also given rise to a new ecosystem of companies offering commercial support and products around open source projects. These companies capitalize on the open source software's popularity by providing additional services, customization, and support, creating new business opportunities and revenue streams. Moreover, open source software has disrupted traditional licensing models by offering free open alternatives.

This has democratized access to software, allowing organizations with limited resources to benefit from powerful tools and technologies. In summary, the open source software movement has sparked innovation, reduced costs, enhanced security, promoted interoperability, and disrupted traditional business models. It continues to shape the software industry, driving collaboration, and benefiting both developers and end-users. Q: How has software testing evolved over time? A: Software testing has undergone significant transformations over the years. Initially, testing was often an afterthought, performed manually and at the end of the development cycle [6]. However, as software complexity increased, and the need for quality assurance became paramount, testing methodologies advanced.

Manual Testing: Initially, testing was primarily done manually, relying on human testers to identify and report issues. Automated Testing: With the rise of scripting languages and testing frameworks, automated testing emerged. This approach allowed for faster and more efficient testing, reducing human effort. Test-Driven Development (TDD): TDD introduced a shift-left approach, where tests are created before writing code. This methodology focuses on writing tests to define expected behavior and then developing code that passes those tests. Continuous Integration and Continuous Testing: The concept of continuous integration (CI) and continuous testing (CT) became popular.

CI involves integrating code changes frequently, while CT ensures that automated tests are executed continuously throughout the development process. Shift-Right Testing: This approach emphasizes testing in production-like environments to identify issues that may arise only in real-world scenarios, enabling organizations to gather valuable feedback and improve the software iteratively. The evolution of software testing methodologies has led to increased efficiency, reduced time to market, and improved software quality. It has also enabled the adoption of Agile and DevOps practices, where testing is an integral part of the development process. References: Fisher, L.

M., & McKenney, J. L. (2007). The PC software industry: Trends, strategies, and contacts. Information Technology & Libraries, 26(1), 18-28. Evans, P., & Wurster, T. S. (2000). Blown to Bits: How the New Economics of Information Transforms Strategy. Harvard Business School Press. Evans, D. (2014). The Internet of Things: How the Next Evolution of the Internet Is Changing Everything. Cisco White Paper. Gartner. (2021). Top Strategic Technology Trends for 2021. Gartner, Inc. Gartner. (2020). Gartner Identifies the Top Strategic Technology Trends for 2020. Gartner, Inc. Kaner, C., Falk, J., & Nguyen, H. Q. (2019). Testing Computer Software. John Wiley & Sons.

Benefits of e-Working

Let's start our training. We start with the following intro. The twenty-first century is a time for the evolution of the information society. Implementing business in electronic form becomes one of the most important criteria for prosperity of the business process. And we can delve into the benefits of e-working. The benefits of e-working are the following. It is working with customers, government and other business entities to promote continued use of information and networking technologies. Digital use reduces or eliminates delays in many business operations from previous actors and from the production/service process to deliver to the end consumer. And there are also the following benefits of e-working. It reduces the business cycle in terms of time for enterprise.

And similarly, through websites, the Internet and corporate networks, information sharing between consumers, manufacturers and suppliers becomes more optimized. E.g. using enterprise networking and cloud computing technologies, customers and business operators can: track their orders, make real-time changes and predict delays in advance. We will follow up with information technology integration. It is the beginning of how information technology should be integrated into the traditional sector of the economy. Their introduction will give momentum to the emergence of new types and ideas for implementing entrepreneurship. Now we're ready for an IT integration strategy model picture.

The first strategy is called consolidation. Its meaning is: it is migrating one entity's IT to the "superior" IT elements of the other. The second strategy is: "preservation". It is about entities retaining most of the unique IT elements and capabilities. For example, the organization has a really nice IT structure, and it maintains it. The third strategy is called "combination". It is selecting the best elements from each IT function to build a new optimized model. The fourth strategy is called "transformation". It is about adopting new systems, processes, provider strategy, technology for new functions.

So it is some kind of antonym of preservation: performing and not on old IT assets, but transforming Into something new. OK. In addition, enterprises in the traditional sector of the economy may face additional threats and opportunities from the process of globalization and the digitization of the international market. And we see in this picture, that industry one dot zero (1.0) was called steam engine. And it was about some first attempts of humanity to build factories and automate at least something. Next come into place mass production lines. It is so-called Industry 2.0.

The third one is about logical systems for automation. And it is the emergence of personal computers, servers for organizations and some kind of computerization of production processes. When we talk about Industry 4.0, it is called the networked intelligent industry. It is the main big goal and it is about digital systems and services platforms. And we see this trend from 2010 to 2020 when enterprises started not only automation of some routine tasks, but some creative tasks are also automated and other features of this kind of industry optimization (comes into production). The next chapter is about the beginning of the 21st century. But that's it for now. I hope to see you soon in the following chapter. Thank you. But that's it for now. And I hope to see you soon in the following chapter. Thank you.

Internet Technologies in 21st Century

We are back with our training. And now it's time to begin with the 21st century, when Internet-related technologies became one of the most significant. They have a tangible impact on most areas of human activity. The business environment is no exception. And we see on this picture that Internet-related technologies are the following: cloud, big data, Blockchain, artificial intelligence that could be applied in many areas. For e.g. management, accounting, financial accounting, audit. But not only stopping on accounting, but on the whole enterprise resource planning areas. All right. And we're ready for the next topic. And it has an impact on the markets.

It has become apparent that the use of web and information and communication technologies, ICT for short, has had a revolutionary impact on the markets of traditional enterprises. Small and medium-sized traditional enterprises are caught up in intense global competition and are now forced to survive in the highly competitive global markets. And of course, after the pandemic, this competition is rising even more and the market is getting tougher. Okay. And in terms of driving forces, we see that it is: social capital, information sharing, information technology, adoption of productivity enhanced technologies. And with some technological progress and developing conditions such as: human resources and their capabilities, opportunities of technologies and efficient work structure and policies.

Companies and the organization would have the following impacts and outcomes of their efforts. It could be improved: product quality and market value, economies of scale, resource use efficiency, productivity improvement, reduced operational cost, improved services to the customer and much more. We can stop the chapter and see the other. Alright. And what about the emergence of a networked environment? The emergence of a networked environment has put pressure on many traditional businesses. It is related to small and medium-sized businesses transforming their business processes.

The transformation was made to meet the needs and demands of the e-business world throughout the use of information and communication technologies. And now let's look at some kind of high-level technical picture about network technologies: from mobile phones to smart devices for digital workers. And enterprise service bus, which is a service for enterprise software or use of cloud technologies and much else. Okay, and now we're ready for an e-business environment. In turn, the e-business environment also brings with it many new prospects to improve, threaten and empower the business processes of traditional enterprises. It expands their real capabilities in each of the transaction acceptance vectors.

It could be business to business - B2B, consumer to business - C2B, business to consumer - B2C, business to employee - B2E and business for government - B2G. The interaction horizon increases in each of these business factors. And now we see that, for example, in B2C transactions, companies use such environments and technologies such as: Facebook, YouTube, Google search and digital advertising, Twitter, email, website, not stopping on these ones, but in increasing such a pool of marketing technologies. And for each of vectors, we see a related pool of technologies and opportunities for enterprises. Alright. Thank you for being with me in this chapter. Hope to see you soon. Bye.

Enterprise Information Flows Upgrade

And where to finish the chapter on digital transformation. We are ready to talk about simplification of enterprise information flow. IT-business processes help speed up and simplify enterprise information flows and provide a tool to enhance the sharing of information and knowledge within and outside the organization. In doing so, they create opportunities to expand and develop new connections between the organization's various departments, as well as its business units and business partners around the world. And what about electronized business processes? They allow geographically disparate exchange participants: manufacturers, suppliers, marketers, end users and others to be a part of a single business process.

In particular, it is about: digitizing metrics of the performance of organization; knowledge assets of corporations and companies, so-called digital universities, cloud universities; tools which are used by employees; monitoring of some metrics and market situation of organization; business processes transformation; techniques used on these enterprises; skills of employees. It's increasing digital plans and how they can be developed. And the planning of the overall strategy and tools of enterprises. And that's it for this chapter. Thank you for being with me, and I hope to see you soon in the next training. Now, thank you and goodbye.

Dear friends, and I want to welcome you to a new topic. And it is a traditional business operation transition to the context of digitization. And, let's start with a quote: "Don't worry about being successful, but work toward being significant and the success will naturally follow." - Oprah Winfrey And we have the following objectives for this training: transition from traditional business operations; today's business challenges of organizations; and new digitized enterprises. For now, dear friends. Thank you for your attention - see you in the training.

ICT as a Transformation System

Dear friends, welcome back. And now let's consider the transition from traditional business operations to the digitization of enterprise business processes. Traditional businesses face 'threats' from an alternative form of business process organization that is used by e-business enterprises. And we see the basic scheme of types of digitization. And it started up from process digitization: starting from converting some analogue documents to digitized ones. Then we have to process digitalization. It is a more complex thing. And after it evolved into digital business transformation. First we will discover in more detail, such aspects.

And now, e-business companies use ICT, which stands for information and communication technologies as a transformation system to a rapidly changing global market. This system allows companies with digitized information processes to get up to date market data, analyze it and make better decisions. And here we have other classes on using IT via organizations. On the IT craftsmanship level we see that focus on technology and the main capabilities are: programming and systems management. And engagement is isolated and it's typically discovered in I.T. departments.

And what about outputs? It's sporadic automation and innovations in some departments, but they're separated and isolated. Next stage is IT industrialization. And focus not on technology this time, but on business processes and its capabilities. It's I.T. management and service management. And colleagues are treated as customers. And in outputs we have services and solutions and the efficiency and effectiveness aspects are considered. And the third stage is digitalization. It is focused on business models and involves digital leadership. And colleagues are treated as partners.

And on outputs we have digital business innovations, new types of business value. In the past, traditional enterprises have responded to changing business environments by saving resources or re-engineering their processes. However, these strategies may not be suitable at the speed of the business cycle and technology upgrades are constantly rising. And businesses are in the rapidly changing business environment now, Where it takes very little time for competitors to move from idea of a product or service to their implementation and production and marketing.

And enterprises face such things as digitized documents; organization of documents in digital form; automation of some processes; streamlining processes in terms of gaining more visibility into operations and increasing efficiency of cross-functional processes. And then transformation of processes, which involve driving innovation by leveraging predictive analytics and insight to transform processes. Dear friends, that's it for this chapter. Next time we will face another of today's business challenges, in terms of business digitization. For now, thank you for your attention.

New Digitized Organizations Tactics

Dear friends, here we are back again. Now it's time to analyze today's business challenges and job transition to digitization. And businesses have relied on analysis of their management activity to solve problems. Organizational knowledge was successfully used at the rate of people who specialized in this particular problem and could solve it. Thus, a certain employee became the source of the answer to a separate question. And sometimes we have such a persona as business analysts. They have manager competency, the worker with project managers in a pair. And they try to become a professional business analyst via CBAP certification.

And they have other relationships, which are deeply involved in business processes with companies and their transformation, while solving the problems. And the interaction of this individual with other people in the organization allowed him to circulate information on the organization. However, today's business challenges are emerging faster than ever, significantly pressuring traditional enterprises, having not only business analysts, but invoking deeper, even deeper into these kinds of problems. This phenomenon also develops to the rate at which market threats and opportunities are emerging.

And for example, enterprises have the following question: are we working too hard, but not very smart? Should we trust our business partners and the Internet and other new types of sources? How important is our website? Can our business become a franchise via Internet activities? There are many traditional companies that cannot operate effectively in a rapidly changing market. They do not have time to adapt to the new requirements and consumer needs of customers as quickly as their competitors.

A classic example of this is a situation with the companies "Borders" and "Barnes and Noble", which overtook Amazon.com through a more accurate and complete strategy of electronization of their business processes. Such marketing and competition of electronic enterprises with traditional ones are typical for other areas of business. Dear friends, we aced this chapter on business challenges and I see you and in the following one on "new digitized enterprises". See you soon.

New Digitized Organizations Tactics

Dear friends, let's now focus on such topics as new digitized enterprises and their tactics. New digitizing enterprises have lower overheads. They can bring products and services to market faster than their traditional competitors. They have achieved this through their creative business models based on information and communication technologies. And, for example, if we have virtual products and virtual production, then they analyze performance data on such things and realize and optimize some collaboration platforms. If they have real products, they try to automate real production via digital twins and analyze digital twins performance.

This novel form of business organization correlates with various e-economic terms, such as e-commerce, e-business, cyber cooperation, digitized business processes, online business, virtual enterprise, cloud learning portal and other virtual forms of organizations. However, they all have some common features such as close relationship with information technology, the Internet, and the ability to collect quickly, process and respond to market situations as soon as possible with the best data. This training also addresses the term "digitized business process" in the context of the corporate and university world. It is integration of the company information systems into a single electronic business system.

And one of the typical systems in such a situation is ERP or enterprise resource planning. And it is the core of the information economic systems. And more recently, we have such things as Cloud Enterprise Resource Planning. It is a cloud version and it can be privately held as a private cloud or public cloud or some variation of two as hybrid cloud: some part of private cloud and public cloud. And in ERP we have such economic aspects under management as inventory, services sales and finance resources and other resources of organization.

And in today's global interaction environment, it is difficult to overestimate the relevance of studying the intercultural component of communication competences among the specialists of organizations. And now it's time to train ourselves in some interactive quiz on the platform and prepare yourself for such questions as: "Performance standards should be ___? Formally discussed; or subjective; or measurable; or significantly challenging. And what about questions such as: "Looking at problems from various points of view helps a small-business owner develop?" Practical arguments; creative solutions; unnecessary conflicts; or unpredictable results.

you can remove some nonsense(worst) scenarios and then you can conduct something and then make the correct choice. And what about question number three. "Yes, you'll save money instantly." It is an example of a statement with ___. Threatening words; an impersonal message; persuasive words; or body language. For now, great job, and see you in the next training.

Economic Function Of Entrepreneurial

Hello, dear friends, and now let's start on topics such as the economic function of entrepreneurial activity. And the term "entrepreneur" is borrowed from the French language. The term is defined as an individual who organizes and operates in one or more types of business. And let's start with such a quote: "All our dreams can come true if we have the courage to pursue them". - Walt Disney. And we have some objectives for this training. It is: giving definition to the term entrepreneurship; to discover entrepreneurial success factors; understand who are project entrepreneurs; discover some details of economics of entrepreneurship and try to understand it entrepreneurial activity. For now, thank you. See you in the next chapters.

Anthony Breer & Entrepreneurship Notions

Dear friends, let's continue our journey. And we'll start with such biographers as Anthony Breer. And he noted that Cantillon saw the entrepreneur as a person taking risks. And the next economist who described entrepreneurs was Sei. And he saw entrepreneurs more as a person planning its economic activities. We see some examples of Richard Cantillon essay on "Economic Theory". And entrepreneurship is a process of starting a business, starting a new company or organization in basic terms. And the entrepreneur develops a business plan, gains human and other necessary sources and takes full responsibility for the success of entrepreneurial business activities.

And we see that the process of entrepreneurial activity involves some kind of innovations, knowledge of entrepreneurship, nice team and assertiveness and risk tolerance. Diving deeper into this term. In recent years the term "entrepreneurship" has broadened its original definition to include social activities also. And entrepreneurship within an existing enterprise or large enterprise is defined as "internal entrepreneurship" and may include management of corporate projects and subsidiaries. For now, that's it - see you in the next chapter.

Entrepreneurs as Business Leaders

Here we go dear friends. And now it's time to understand such a topic as "entrepreneurs as business leaders". And entrepreneurs are business leaders willing to take risks and take risks and take the initiative to take advantage of market opportunities through: planning, organizing it and using resources. Often by introducing innovative or improving existing products and services. More recently, the term "entrepreneurship" has been further deepened. And has begun to include a certain type of thinking aimed at social activism and expansion and promotion of knowledge and human values. And we remember some things from the previous chapters on this topic.

And the whole entrepreneurial framework will influence company mission, business model, strategy and goals on the top. And in the middle architecture of business, data architecture, application architecture and technological infrastructure. If we have some sophisticated technological company. And entrepreneurial activity differs depending on the type of organization and the degree of creative activity. Entrepreneurial activity ranges from one person and temporary projects in large enterprises to the creation of numerous permanent jobs. What about the entrepreneurial framework? This framework includes such things as entrepreneurial finance, cultural, social norms, government programs, legal and commercial infrastructure, government policy, physical infrastructure, entrepreneurship education, market openness and so on.

These factors will influence entrepreneurship and it is called entrepreneurial framework conditions. What about a new enterprise? It is also called startups. They seek to attract third-party capital or business angels to finance and expand their business. These are organizations (business angels type) that support potential:

entrepreneurs, specialized government bodies, business incubators, science parks and some non-governmental organizations. That's it for this chapter, see you in the next one.

Entrepreneurial Success Factors

Welcome back, dear friends. And now it's time for such topics as entrepreneurial success factors. Entrepreneurial success factors include activity within different environments. The market environment, for example, assumes the following things: effective business model choices. These models could be: business to business, business to consumer, business to government. And high market growth and also working with target customers. What about the industrial environment of entrepreneurial activity? This environment includes the following: Choosing an industry with growth prospects. High-impact of technology on the industry.

Low capital investment. Small average size of the existing firm. If we dive deep into the entrepreneurial ecosystem, we see such factors as: human capital, workforce, education and training involved. Universities as catalysts of entrepreneurial activity. Mentor advisors and support systems. Culture of entrepreneurship. Funding and finance are also parts of the entrepreneurial ecosystem. And one of the most important things of entrepreneurship is working with teams. And this activity involves the following: Teams from a variety of specialists are needed, as well as specialists with different qualifications, experiences, skills in starting new businesses. And successful entrepreneurial experience.

And the number and variety of social connections of team members are also implied. What about team activities? These activities could involve such things as: holiday events, gift exchanges, workshops, icebreaker questions and volunteer days. The organization puts forward a number of demands. It could be creating a quality business plan; entrepreneurial activity should focus on one product/service; intensive marketing activity on these products should be organized. That's it for the topic of entrepreneurial success factors in general. In the following chapters we will discover other aspects of entrepreneurial activity. See you.

Project Entrepreneurs

Here we go, dear friends. And now it's time for such topics as project entrepreneurs. And the project entrepreneurs or project managers are individuals who are engaged in the management of organizations. These organizations have a limited life cycle dedicated to solving a particular problem. Achieving a goal that ends with a certain result. The market sectors where project management is widespread include music, information technologies and new media industries. A feature of project management from a theoretical point of view is the need for its timely adaptation to market conditions by switching to new business opportunities.

As a practice result of this activity, project managers are addressing the challenges and inherent such challenges in the business process. Project managers face two critical challenges that invariably characterize the creation of a new organization: The first, it is discovering the right opportunity to start an enterprise project. And the second, hiring the most appropriate team to make effective use of these business opportunities. Solving the first task requires the project manager to process a wide range of information necessary to take advantage of innovation and investment business opportunities.

Solving the second task requires a team that has good skills to deal with specific project issues and must be ready to function effectively immediately to reduce the risk of performance degradation. Solving this task project manager needs some kind of skills. And these skills include such as: leadership, communication, risk management, critical thinking, quality management and of course, a sense of humor. Many businesses need more capital than owners have available in the situation. In which case the range of options available to get some funds from: business angels, venture capitalist, or financing hedge funds and alternative asset management.

And some of these sources provide not only funds, but also financial control over usage of such funds. Accountability for effective implementation of tasks and stages of the project. In some cases business contacts and - often in exchange for a stake in the company. That's it for the project entrepreneurs topic. See you in the next chapter.

Economics of Entrepreneurship

Hello, dear friends, and let's continue with such a topic as "economics of entrepreneurship. The economics of membership is a study of business activity and entrepreneurs in the economy. The accumulation of factors of production as such does not explain the economic development. They are considered necessary in production, but only their availability will not be sufficient for economic growth. And here comes into play such a thing as creative activity. And it is an activity that leads to the creation of new knowledge and the transformation of it into goods before consumer demand.

And efficient entrepreneurship is necessary with creative activity to synthesize economic resources in a profitable way. As well as an institutional environment that encourages entrepreneurship through people. This is decisive for economic growth. Thus, entrepreneurial activity is central to explaining the phenomenon of long-term economic development and growth. In the early stages of economic business theory, however, due attention was not paid to such things. And we want to understand the entrepreneurship life-cycle. At the very beginning, it is potentially entrepreneurs.

Then it is intentional entrepreneurs. And after it they can start the process of new business or so-called startup entrepreneurship. Then they become owners of established businesses. And in the 6th stage they stop running business. Or become so-called discontinued entrepreneurs. That's it, dear friends, for this chapter. And I see you soon in the following one.

Entrepreneurial Activity Notion

And we continue our journey on entrepreneurial activity. And entrepreneurial activity is economic activity aimed at systematically profiting from the production and/or sale of goods and services. And entrepreneurial activity remains more important to the economy than ever before. While classical economics requires further research on such topics. The characteristics of an economy with a sufficient level of entrepreneurial activity should be a high level of innovation. It should be combined with a high level of entrepreneurship that leads to the creation of new organizations, as well as new industries. Thus, entrepreneurial activity can be defined as a dynamic indicator of the realization of entrepreneurial potential in the current business climate. This interpretation of entrepreneurial activity allows not only to assess the current state of business activity in the real sector of the economy. But also to draw a conclusion about the dynamics of changes in business activity.

As well as trends of increasing or decrease in the activity of business structures of the real sector of the economy. And now if we see some maps of the best and worst entrepreneurship regions in 2018. E.g. in North America the leader is the United States, and Mexico has the worst position in this region. It is positioned #74 worldwide. And what about South America? Chile is one of the leaders with 19th place and Venezuela is the worst one in the region. And what about Europe? Then Switzerland, it's #2 worldwide and leader here. And on the bottom place is Bosnia-Herzegovina #94 and so on. We see some other leaders such as Australia and Israel. And that's it for this chapter. See you soon.

Approaches to Entrepreneurship Analysis

Here we go, and now it's time to continue our journey on entrepreneurial activities. And as we remember, entrepreneurship is difficult to analyze via traditional economic tools. Such mathematical analysis methods and general equilibrium models. But it is opposed to general theoretical scientific and philosophical methods, which are not in analyzing entrepreneurial activity. And modern textbooks of economic theory only casually mention the concepts of entrepreneurial activity and the role of entrepreneurs in the economy. Research on entrepreneurial activity in the economy is largely one of the four main schools of thought. Early economists such as Max Weber noted the emergence of the term "entrepreneurship" in the context of religious belief. Thus suggesting that some belief systems discourage entrepreneurial activity. This statement, however, has been challenged by many socialist-economists.

Some thinkers, such as Samuelson, for example, believed that there was no link between religion, economic development and entrepreneurship. But Karl Marx, in turn, considered the economic system and the way of production as the only factors of economic development. Weber instead suggested that there was a direct link between ethics and the economic system, as they interact intensively. We see different views on one topic via different economists. Dear friends, that's it. See you in the next chapter.

Frank Knight & J. Schumpeter Concepts

Welcome back, dear friends. And now, it's time to analyze different definitions of "entrepreneur". Let's start with a definition of Frank Nye and he defined Intrapreneur as someone who takes responsibility for business decisions in uncertainty. Uncertainty in Knight understanding exists where there is no basis for calculated, objective probabilities. So it is immeasurable and decisions must be made using subjective judgments. The entrepreneur earns economic benefits as a reward for correct judgments. And entrepreneurs are also seen as confident and risk averse individuals. And another view on definition is from Schumpeter's concept, which is manifested in the synthesis of three different definitions of an entrepreneur.

The first as a risk taker, the second as innovator, and the third as a manager. Schumpeter assigned the role of innovator to entrepreneur, believing that economic growth arises from the process of creative destruction. And not through capitalist iterations. And capitalist support capital, and entrepreneurs create innovations. And we see that 'innovations' were further developed in Schumpeter theory into the kinds of categories such as: technological innovation, organizational innovation, institutional innovation and social innovation. According to Schumpeter, an entrepreneur is considered only the economic agent who carries out the new business activity.

And he loses that status as soon as business is built and the agent starts working and running the enterprise like everyone else. The emphasis here is not on the categories of personas, but also on their functions. And to sum up, the entrepreneur, according to Schumpeter, disturbs the existing balance in the market. And innovation is chaos, an unpredictable economic process that cannot be modeled on the basis of equilibrium analytical methods of economics used in classical economic theory. That's it for this chapter. In the next one we will further delve into the definition of entrepreneurial activity. See you.

Kirzner, Baumol and Leibenstein Concepts

Dear friends and we're back. And now It's time to understand the definition of intrapreneur by Israel Kirzner. And he saw entrepreneurs as an intermediary of banking and trading operations. Entrepreneur is one integral who's ready for the profit opportunities that exist due to lack of market equilibrium. Lack of equilibrium of supply and demand. Another one definition of entrepreneurial activity is a creative response to inefficiency. This definition is according to Harvey Leibenstein. And entrepreneurs are also considered as 'repeaters' with the ability to perceive market opportunities and develop innovative goods or services that are not currently delivered.

And the contribution of Leibenstein is: "Entrepreneurship as the reduction of organizational inefficiency." And this economist argues that entrepreneurs have a special opportunity to connect markets and compensate for market weaknesses. In addition, based on the theories of Saye and Cantillon Leibenstein suggests that entrepreneurs have the opportunity to combine different economic resources into innovations in order to meet unrealized market demand. And one more great economist is Baumol, who argued that entrepreneurship can be productive or unproductive. Entrepreneurs can carry out economically legitimate activities or some kind of non-lawful activities.

Societies differ significantly in the way they define entrepreneurial activity between two forms of entrepreneurship. Depending on existing rules of the game, such as laws in each individual society. We can also give our own definition of entrepreneurial activity. And it is proposed to define entrepreneurial activity in the context of an internet business environment, for example, which is designated as an open system of network transactions, which are characterized by the process of information and knowledge exchange of players in the internal and external economic spaces. And it transformed under the influence of international business experience.

And we see that technology can be upgraded in enterprises from traditional proprietary technologies with Internet integration and then with full back-office integration of Internet and cloud technologies, in the brief. Dear friends, that's it for entrepreneurial activity definitions. And now it's time to prepare ourselves for the quiz. You could face the following questions on the interactive quiz. For example, what is a business that conducts business by means of the Internet? It is online business - A. Service business - B. Home based business - C. Green business - D. Another question which you could find is: "which of the following is a current business trend?" A. It services business Social entrepreneurship, outsourcing or all the above. What about one more thing?

l and _____ is an intangible thing that businesses do for us that enhance our lives. A. Good B. Supply or C. service or D. demand. And make attention to what intangible is. And this is the clue for this question. And the question number four: "Entrepreneur who recognizes a social problem and uses entrepreneurial methods to improve society A. home based entrepreneur B. web based entrepreneur C. social entrepreneur D. Traditional entrepreneur. Dear friends, I wish you have fun and some experience on making answers in this quiz. Well done. So you in the next training.

Unlocking Capital and Success Factors for Entrepreneurial Growth

This paper explores the different avenues available to secure capital for your business, such as business angels, venture capitalists, co-financing, hedge funds, and alternative asset management. It delves into the success factors within market and industrial environments, emphasizing the significance of a capable and diverse team. Moreover, it sheds light on how entrepreneurial activity propels economic growth and highlights the intricacies and definitions surrounding entrepreneurship in today's business landscape. Gain valuable insights into the transformative power of entrepreneurial activity, particularly in the internet business environment.

Keywords: Secure capital for business; Venture capitalists; Success factors in market and industrial environments; Capable and diverse team; Economic growth and entrepreneurship; Definitions of entrepreneurship; Internet business environment Unveiling the Power of Entrepreneurs: Catalysts of Innovation, Competition, and Economic Growth The theory of economic functions of entrepreneurial activity explores the role and impact of entrepreneurs in the business world. The term "entrepreneur" originated from the French language and refers to individuals who organize and operate one or more businesses.

It is credited to the French economist Jean-Baptiste Saye for popularizing the term, while the Irish economist Richard Cantillon had previously defined the concept in his essay on the general nature of trade [1]. Cantillon viewed entrepreneurs as risk-takers, whereas Saye portrayed entrepreneurs as individuals who strategically plan their economic activities. Entrepreneurship encompasses the process of starting new businesses or organizations. Entrepreneurs develop comprehensive business plans, acquire the necessary resources, and bear full responsibility for the success or failure of their venture.

Entrepreneurial activities take place within the business environment, where entrepreneurs navigate the dynamics of markets, competition, and consumer demands. In recent years, the concept of enterprise has broadened to include social activities. Entrepreneurship within existing enterprises or large organizations is referred to as "internal entrepreneurship," which involves managing corporate projects and subsidiaries. Entrepreneurs are visionary leaders who are willing to take risks and seize market opportunities through effective planning, organizing, and resource utilization. They often introduce innovative products or improve existing ones, aiming to meet the evolving needs and demands of customers.

It is important to note that entrepreneurship plays a significant role in driving economic growth, job creation, and innovation. Entrepreneurs are central to fostering competition, driving productivity, and shaping industries. Their ability to promote economic development has been well-documented, with studies indicating a positive correlation between entrepreneurial activity and economic performance. In conclusion, entrepreneurial activity is a multifaceted process that involves individuals who take risks and lead businesses with the aim of capitalizing on market opportunities. Entrepreneurs play a crucial role in driving innovation, fostering competition, and propelling economic growth.

From Profit to Purpose: The Expanding Horizons of Entrepreneurship Entrepreneurial activity has evolved to encompass various dimensions, including social activism and the promotion of knowledge and human values. Today, entrepreneurship extends beyond purely profit-oriented ventures, with a growing emphasis on creating social impact and advancing societal well-being [2]. The nature of entrepreneurial activity varies based on the type of organization and the level of innovation involved. This spectrum ranges from individual entrepreneurs working on temporary projects within large enterprises to the establishment of numerous permanent job opportunities. Start-up ventures often seek external funding from sources like venture capitalists or angel investors to support their growth and expansion.

In addition, there are numerous organizations dedicated to supporting aspiring entrepreneurs, including government bodies, business incubators, science parks, and non-governmental organizations. Project entrepreneurs, also known as project managers, are individuals responsible for managing temporary organizations. These organizations have a limited lifespan and are focused on addressing specific challenges or achieving predefined goals. Industries such as music, media, software development, construction, and new media commonly rely on project management frameworks. One notable aspect of project management is its adaptability to market conditions, enabling project managers to seize new business opportunities as they arise.

This entrepreneurial activity involves addressing and overcoming the challenges inherent in the business process. Project managers face two crucial tasks in establishing a new enterprise: identifying the right opportunity to undertake a project and assembling an effective team to capitalize on this business opportunity. The first task requires project managers to process a wide array of information to identify innovative ideas and investment opportunities. Effectively solving the second task necessitates building a skilled team capable of tackling the specific challenges of the project and being ready to perform optimally from the outset, minimizing the risk of performance degradation.

Entrepreneurial success relies on the ability to identify and seize opportunities while assembling teams equipped with the necessary expertise. By navigating these challenges, project managers and entrepreneurs can forge new paths, drive innovation, and contribute to economic and social growth. Unlocking Capital and Success Factors: The Path to Entrepreneurial Growth Businesses often require more capital than their owners have readily available. In such cases, there are various options to consider, including: Business angels: These are individual investors who provide capital and expertise to early-stage or growing companies in exchange for an equity stake.

Venture capitalists: Venture capital firms invest in high-growth potential startups and provide funding, guidance, and connections in exchange for equity. They typically focus on innovative and scalable business models. Co-financing: This involves securing funds from multiple sources, such as combining equity investment from business angels with loans or grants from government programs or financial institutions. Hedge funds: Hedge funds are pools of capital from accredited investors, which can provide high-risk financing options for businesses in need of capital. Alternative asset management: This refers to various institutional investors, such as private equity firms or pension funds, that manage non-traditional assets and can provide funding to businesses.

These sources of funding not only offer financial support but can also bring added value in the form of financial oversight, task implementation accountability, business contacts, and experience. However, they often require a stake in the company in return. Successful entrepreneurship relies on various factors within different environments. In the market environment, key factors include making effective business model choices (B2B, B2C, or B2G), operating in high-growth markets, and effectively engaging with target customers [3]. In the industrial environment, factors for success include selecting industries with growth prospects, recognizing the impact of technology on the industry, requiring low capital investment, and operating in industries with smaller average-sized existing firms.

Working with a capable and diverse team is also essential for entrepreneurial success. Factors such as having a team composed of specialists with diverse qualifications, prior management experience, experience in launching new businesses, successful track records of entrepreneurship, motivation driven by potential profits, and a substantial number and variety of social connections among team members all contribute to a strong foundation for success.

The Demands and Impact of Entrepreneurial Activity in Economic Growth

The organization of entrepreneurial endeavors necessitates certain demands and considerations. These include: Creating a quality business plan: A well-crafted business plan serves as a roadmap for entrepreneurial activities and outlines strategies for success. Focus on one product or service: Concentrating efforts on a single offering enables entrepreneurs to achieve specialization and excellence in their chosen field. Intensive marketing activity: Robust marketing efforts are crucial for promoting products or services, reaching target audiences, and achieving business growth. Tight financial management: Effective financial management ensures optimal allocation of resources, cash flow management, and profitability.

The study of entrepreneurship and its economic implications reveals that the mere accumulation of factors of production does not suffice in explaining economic development. While these factors are essential for production, economic growth necessitates creative activity, the conversion of knowledge into marketable goods, efficient entrepreneurship, and an institutional environment that fosters free enterprise. Entrepreneurial activity plays a pivotal role in driving long-term economic development and growth. However, early economic theories did not adequately emphasize its significance [4]. Thus, further research is required to enhance our understanding of entrepreneurship within the realm of classical economic theory.

An economy characterized by a heightened entrepreneurial activity exhibits a combination of high innovation levels and the establishment of new enterprises and industries. Such activity serves as a dynamic indicator of entrepreneurial potential realization in the current business climate. This interpretation allows us to not only assess the present state of business activity in the real sector of the economy, but also draw conclusions about trends, changes, and the overall activity of business entities within the real sector. Exploring the Complexities and Definitions of Entrepreneurship Entrepreneurship is a multifaceted concept that poses challenges to traditional economic analysis.

Mathematical and equilibrium models, commonly used in economic theory, often struggle to capture the essence of entrepreneurial activity [5]. Mainstream textbooks tend to provide only brief mentions of entrepreneurship and the role of entrepreneurs in the economy. Early economists, such as Max Weber, associated the term "enterprise" with religious belief systems and suggested that certain ideologies discourage entrepreneurial activity. However, this perspective has been contested by sociologist-economists who argue against a direct link between religion, economic development, and entrepreneurship.

Scholars like Samuelson challenged the connection, while Karl Marx focused on economic systems and modes of production as the primary drivers of development. Weber, on the other hand, suggested a direct interaction between ethics and the economic system [5]. Frank Knight defined entrepreneurs as individuals who shoulder the responsibility of making business decisions in situations of uncertainty. Knight's understanding of uncertainty refers to scenarios where objective probabilities cannot be calculated, requiring subjective judgments. Entrepreneurs, characterized as confident and risk-averse, are rewarded with economic benefits for making correct judgments.

Joseph Schumpeter's concept of entrepreneurship combines three distinct roles: risk-taker, innovator, and manager. Schumpeter emphasized the entrepreneur's role in driving economic growth through the process of creative destruction rather than traditional capitalist operations. According to Schumpeter, the entrepreneur's status is temporary, dissolved once the business is established and the agent assumes their regular functions [6]. This perspective emphasizes the functions performed by individuals rather than categorizing them.

Schumpeter argued that entrepreneurs disrupt existing equilibrium and bring about innovation, which is an unpredictable and chaotic economic process. This perspective challenges the applicability of equilibrium-based analytical methods used in classical economic theory. Israel Kirzner, an economist from the Austrian School, viewed entrepreneurs as intermediaries engaging in banking and trading operations, capitalizing on profit opportunities resulting from market disequilibrium [7]. Harvey Leibenstein, an American economist, saw entrepreneurial activity as a creative response to inefficiency.

Entrepreneurs were considered "repeaters" with a unique ability to identify market opportunities and develop innovative goods or services that are not currently available. Leibenstein posited that entrepreneurs have the capacity to connect markets and address market deficiencies. Drawing on the theories of J. B. Say and Richard Cantillon, he suggested that entrepreneurs combine economic resources to create innovative solutions that meet unrealized market demand [8]. Baumol, an American economist, categorized entrepreneurship as productive or unproductive and highlighted that entrepreneurs can engage in legitimate or criminal activities.

Societies vary in how they define and perceive entrepreneurial activity, influenced by their specific rules and regulations [9]. In the context of the internet business environment, entrepreneurial activity can be defined as an open system of network transactions characterized by the exchange of information and knowledge within internal and external economic spaces. This activity is shaped by international business experiences and the transformative power of digital connectivity. Conclusion: The Transformative Nature of Entrepreneurial Activity in the Internet Business Environment Entrepreneurial activity in the internet business environment is a transformative force, shaping the way economic transactions occur in the digital sphere.

This open system of network transactions is characterized by the exchange of information and knowledge, both within internal networks and with external economic spaces. It is influenced by the experiences and practices of international businesses, paving the way for innovative approaches and remarkable growth opportunities. The internet has transformed the entrepreneurial landscape, providing unprecedented opportunities for businesses to connect, collaborate, and leverage digital platforms for their ventures. Let's explore some examples, facts, data, and insights: E-commerce boom: The rise of online marketplaces, such as Amazon and Alibaba, has enabled entrepreneurs to reach global audiences and tap into previously untapped markets.

In 2020, global e-commerce sales amounted to a staggering $4.28 trillion, a clear indication of the immense potential for entrepreneurial success in the digital realm [10]. Tech startups and unicorns: The internet has given birth to numerous technology startups that have quickly scaled to become billion-dollar companies, known as "unicorns." These ventures, like Airbnb and Uber, have disrupted traditional industries and transformed the way we travel, book accommodations, and use transportation services. As of 2021, there are over 800 unicorns worldwide, with a combined valuation of over $2.6 trillion [11]. Crowdfunding and access to capital: Online crowdfunding platforms, such as Kickstarter and Indiegogo, have democratized access to capital for aspiring entrepreneurs.

Through these platforms, individuals can showcase their innovative ideas and raise funds from a vast network of potential backers. In 2020, global crowdfunding campaigns raised over $17 billion, providing crucial support to entrepreneurs across various industries [12]. Remote work and digital entrepreneurship: The internet has enabled flexible working arrangements and has fueled the rise of digital entrepreneurship. More individuals are embracing remote work, allowing them to start their own online businesses and work from anywhere in the world. This shift has opened up new opportunities and expanded the pool of entrepreneurial talent globally.

Knowledge and information sharing: The internet serves as a vast repository of knowledge and resources, empowering entrepreneurs to learn, acquire new skills, and stay updated with industry trends. Online communities, forums, and educational platforms offer valuable insights, mentorship, and networking opportunities, fostering an environment conducive to entrepreneurial growth.

Evolution of IT Business

Hello, dear friends, and now it's time to understand the following theme: "Essentials of IT-business transformation" and we start with a quote and today's quote is the following: "Be the change you wish to see in the world." - Mahatma Gandhi. And we have the following objectives to work on today: the evolution of business activity; virtual representations on the Internet for enterprises; the history of the entrepreneurial part of the Internet and those objectives and some details and further understanding we will see in the following chapters. For now - thank you. See you.

Here we go dear friends. And now it's time to see the following theme. It is an evolution of business activity. And the evolution of business activity towards the growth of electronic business functions began with the use of computers in the 1980s and the development of the Internet and its commercial aspect in the 1990s. The latest trends in e-business are the transition to mobile and cloud (network services), as well as big data since the 2010s and artificial intelligence technologies. And we can see top topics of information technologies in 2020: 5G technologies, cloud-based services and its evolution; IOT integration; and IoT it is Internet of Things; agile practices in IT-industry and other industries; robotic process automation and other.

What about the evolution of IT-businesses, it has allowed industries to expand the data from paper media to store an extensive amount of digital variation on enterprise services. Electronic data technologies have allowed businesses to increase both storage and the data processing speed. And this technology allows companies to improve its storage and review the whole process from standard Media and creating via I.T. technologies and integrating scheduling into the digital environment. Prognosis, which was done mainly with the help of computing, began to be faster and better with the active use of spreadsheets and special computer programs.

Businesses began storing computer interaction data electronically and could quickly access the data in real time. And on the whole, information technology allows companies to effectively use the Internet; tries to be secure, support its operations, improve some systems of businesses, use network capacity for business needs, and allow the development of a unique system of organizations to implement it for efficiencies in the market. And the Internet has become a key technology for e-business. By growing from a military and educational network to commercial network in the early 1990s, the Internet became the basis for virtual representations of e-commerce organizations and businesses.

And let's briefly look at the history of the Internet and we see some creation of WebTrends in 1993, creation of Analog in 1995, Web-Counter in 1996, Creating Java technology in 1997, and associated companies with them; starting from some Micro-systems and then selling Java to Oracle Corporation. And of course, 2005. And the launch of Google Trends and Analytics; and Mobile Analytics after 2010 comes into place; and many other aspects of Internet evolution. What about the history of the entrepreneurial part of the Internet? And its history: one of the major points are 1994 the development of Netscape browser and the war with Microsoft Explorer in those years; then it was the founding of Amazon and eBay in 1995; and the opening of PayPal: an Internet payment company, which was organized in 1998. That's it, dear friends. Next time we will understand virtual representation of organizations on the Internet. Now, thank you. See you.

Mobile Communication Evolution

Here we are dear friends and now let's understand, such as the Internet. Well, major international enterprises have virtual representations on the Internet by 2020, many of them sell goods and services directly at their online offices. And what about the number of Internet users in 2020? We have four billion connected people. It is about a four trillion revenue opportunity. For now, 25 million apps are ready and 25 billion embedded and intelligence systems are developed and 50 trillion gigabytes of data. And it is another big topic to be discovered. It is big data and related to the Internet of Things and others.

But now with the development of the Internet and small businesses that don't have their own and that representation are beginning to walk in this direction, and we see such Internet business companies such as eBay, Google, Yahoo, Amazon and traditional enterprises like Honda and other car makers and agencies, investment related companies from banks like Deutsche Bank and others to enterprises like Microsoft, Intel. Samsung and others. What about mobile? Mobile is a big trend in Internet and Internet commerce, with mobile devices generating more and more Internet traffic, websites are becoming more optimized for mobile devices and mobile apps.

It allows owners of smartphones and tablets to access the information they are interested in. in more widely via the I.T. business suits for mobile. And we see things becoming more and more like payment, which are now from mobile devices, which are usually discovered in the China market, but not very well. For now in Western countries; information and content services from standard web based apps are becoming more and more available for mobile devices starting from Internet access to search engines, Useful navigation. For now, these chapters, music. games, TV and communication standards for phones and also the upgrading of mobile standards from SMS, MMS, 3G, 4G and 5G nonstop there.

New electronic technologies have made it possible to transform traditional business communication in the shortest time. E-business communication has developed from traditional posting technology and fax to email fastly, to IP telephony and chapter conferencing. For e.g. rise of Zoom. And VIber before it and so on. And international telephone communication has become significantly cheaper because of Internet protocol with technologies. It is IP telephony in the short term and started with Skype from 2003 and with Viber in 2010. Google Hand Out in 2013; Telegram Technologies in 2013; Microsoft for Teams in 2017 for business segment.

And not stopping with this list. And now, dear friends, let's prepare ourselves for our quiz on the introduction from here. Using ICT in business involves. That is a question you will face: A. Strategies to select hardware and software systems, or ethical and socially responsible management or implications of the use of technology or all of the above. Make your choice in interaction societies after this chapter. The second question you will face, one of the most important financial management is to ensure that technological systems are secured for all market niches or none of them are above.

Read for some clues and so on. Issues involving computer use involve: identity fraud, cyber bullying, unauthorized hackers access to system, all of the above. Some understanding or basic information technologies will be nice to have to answer this, but, keep trying and have fun with this question; and question them for investment in technology can result in: cost savings by having fewer employees, higher training costs, having a maintenance budget to keep the equipment up to date or all of the above. And that's the fourth question for you to try your skills.

For now dear friends. I was very happy for you to be with you and well done. See you in the next training session.

Management Notion

Dear friends, welcome to another chapter regarding some project management activities, and we introduce you with a quote, and the quote is from Michael Jordan, NBA Hall of Famer, and it is the following: "I failed over and over again in my life and that's why I succeed." So let's move forward to another thing in this topic and it is regarding the objectives of this training. And we have the following objectives. So we should discover the management, the concept and the essence in order to solidify our knowledge in this area. Then the computational thinking concept comes into place.

Some management principles, project management concepts, key project management methodologies will be introduced to you in more details: from agile families, scrum, kanban and Lean and also waterfall methodology. Also, scrum planning, kanban essence and features will be introduced to you. For now dear friends thank you for being with me. See you in the following chapter.

We continue our journey on the introduction to project management and after discovering the objectives of the training we should warm up to this topic. After warming up we should discover the following theme. And it is a definition of management concept. And management in one form or another has always existed in human life where people worked in groups and, as a rule, for spheres of human society, it could be the following subdivision as political, economic and other fields and functions of human society. In politics, it is the need to establish and maintain order in the groups. In the economy It is necessary to find, produce and allocate resources for society. And in defense: it is protection from enemies and wild beasts. So management, as a rule, exists in each area. Okay, dear friends, and after discovering such an introduction, we are ready for the following topic. On project management and in particular, its introduction, See you soon.

Management Theory Evolution

Welcome back. This chapter will be dedicated to project management evolution. We start with the first period. It is a period of management evolution. The first simplest rudimentary forms of ordering and organization of joint work existed at the stage of the primitive communal system of society. And that time the management was carried out jointly by all members of the society or family of those tribes, or communities. Elders and leaders of families and tribes represented the guiding principle of all activities of that period. So that concludes the first period. And we are ready to move to the second period.

And it is called the ancient period. And it is regarding 9 to 7 thousand years before Christ to the 18th century. And the famous figures from that period are Sócrates, Plato, and Alexander the Great, starting with Alexander the Great and is some kind of Macedonian great war chief and commander. Which developed the theory and practice of troop management in those ancient times. And he performed very well and established very many colonies. And then we should mention such figures and philosophers as Plato. Plato gave a classification of forms, government and tried to distinguish between the functions of government. Another one is Socrates. Socrates analyzed various forms of government on the basis of which proclaimed the principle of universal management. All right. Moving to the following period. And now it is a period of systematization.

In particular from 1856 to 1960. The modern concept of management was during the industrial revolution of the 19th century. The emergence of the factory as a primary type of production and the need to provide work for large groups of people meant that individual owners could no longer observe the activities of all workers. Because that is where we introduced many people from villages to the cities. And one man, one owner could not fully support each process and each man, which was his worker, Owners trained, the best workers trained so that they could represent themselves and the interests of their owners in the workplace or in the factory. And they were the first managers.

All right, let's move further. It is the 4th period: informational period. And from 1960 to the present moment. Later management theories were developed mainly by representatives of the quantitative school that is often called management. And the appearance of this school is the consequences of the use of mathematics and computers in management practices. So from the name quantitative schools. Use of measurements, use of computers and such practices. Such school representatives see management as a logical process that can be expressed in Mathematics. The formalization of a number of management functions, the combination of labor, men, and computers, required a review of the structural elements of the organization in subdivisions such as accounting, marketing.

All right, let's move on further. It's time for a second informational period and some additional topics. on informational period. This is about new elements of intercompany planning, which have emerged. Such as simulation of solutions, methods of analysis in uncertain conditions, mathematical provision of multipurpose management decisions evaluation. All right. Alright, and this concludes this chapter on project management evolution. Thank you for your attention. See you in the following chapter.

System Approach

Welcome back. This chapter will be dedicated to topics such as system approach, Project management practices and ideas from computational thinking will be introduced for you. And what about system approach? This approach assumes that leaders should use the organization as a set of interconnected parts. These parts are: people; structure; tasks; technology and resources. The main idea of system theory is the following: that no action is taken in isolation from other action in the system. Each decision has implications for the whole system. Each system part has implications on another part of the system.

Thinking Process in Computer Science

In the last chapter, we introduced some kind of system approach for you. And now it's time for concepts such as computational thinking. And when we talk about the programming language, then this kind of structure allows us to explain to computers how to execute a particular solution to some problem in real life. And first an IT specialist has to come up with a solution also using a skill which is mandatory for any type of programming no matter the language. And it is called computational thinking. So the first is that logic of some programming comes into place and then the programmer could use the particular codes and structures of the programming language. And computers can only deal with clear, concise instructions that agree with the rules of formal logic. However real world problems rarely cut so precisely.

Computational thinking is a set of mental skills that can help programmers and other I.T. specialists to see the problems and the set of compound information processes, which could be transformed into a particular set of instructions for a computer, which can be implemented. And let's now move a little bit further. And after introducing the computational thinking, we should solidify its understanding in the following concept. So moving to the following. Computational thinking is a simple algorithm, and this algorithm should do the following things. First of all, it should describe the problem.

Then identify the essential details in this problem. After it decomposes the parts. And connect the pieces. And test the whole process. If we talk about describing a problem we should understand what exactly needs to be done, What input data is given, and what does the desired outcome look like? Well, part of the essential details identification comes into place. Some I.T. specialists needed to solve such problems.

Before thinking of a solution you should make sure to consider all the important aspects of the problem. The devil as the proverb says is in the detail.

And in the case of programming, it lies in boundary cases. And this in particular is important for quality assurance as a part of a software development. And what about the decompose stage? It is breaking the program into smaller ones from the huge ones. And logical steps until knowing exactly how to code each part. Using these steps to create an algorithm will help to solve the issue. And connecting the pieces after the composing stage to produce the desired outcome and system, in the system approach, in all specified cases. After it the process could be tested. And usually, a problem has at least a few solutions. And it's very useful to elevate some ideas to make sure that the most efficient solution is chosen. It's alright.

And since computational thinking is a skill it requires a lot of practice before it could be applied. And no need to sorrow if only thought when looking at the problem is that there is no idea how to achieve the desired result. And it's a common practice. Using the algorithm described could help to break the problem into solvable parts until you could see you progress in this solution. And could help you all the way or your teammates according to your project terms. Alright dear friends and that's it for this chapter on computational thinking. It was more in the context of business analysis in IT and the introduction to project management. See you in the following ones.

Management Process

Welcome to this chapter dedicated to management work. We discussed such things as project management evolution, some specific computational thinking in I.T. area. We are now ready to solidify our understanding of what management is. With some definition of a modern one. And It is the planning, organization, motivation, and control processes needed to shape and achieve the organization goals. It is a type of public work whose main task is to ensure that purposeful, coordinated activities of both individual participants in the joint work process and the workforce as a whole. Alright, that's it for a definition of management, and there are features of managerial work.

They are the following: There are some results and some means by which these results are attained. Labor subject information and participation In mental work. If we are talking about mental work then it is organizational. administrative and educational work of a manager. Analysis and construction of processes and I.T. related projects. And participation is a creation of material goods not directly, but indirectly by some given tasks and so on. And the means of work are organizational and computing equipment nowadays. As a result it is a management decision. And what about the famous "Plan -> -> Do -> Check -> Act" cycle. We have some kind of planning activities. How should some features be implemented? Then doing this, what to do and how to do it.

And checking it for some control. So what has been achieved in these stages after doing the act? Act comes into place and what is still to be done. How should we act further? Once again, planning, doing, checking, and acting on the following target. So that's the basic steps in project management and managerial work. What about the planning stage? Regarding the team, the road map of the project should be different for web-team it could be: admin consoles, for example, implementation, or security principles implementing, some encryption and so on. And so for mobile, it could be working on user experience, some tapping activities and gestures on mobile devices.

The marketing team could be doing another product roadmap planning For example, a marketing analysis, search engine option, optimization plans for organic search, for example, paid advertisement and so on. So it should be, of course, industry specific. And what about organizations? This step ensures there's a technical, economic, social, psychological, and also legal aspect of organization activities that are streamlined to possible maximum outcome. If the planning function answers the question of what. What to include, what to do or planning what to do. Then The organization's function raises questions about who and how we will implement these steps from the planning stage. I.e. who and how. Alright.

Moving forward. We are moving forward with motivation's steps. After planning and organization, we should find motivation for our employees and teammates. And by definition, motivation is a process of encouraging yourself and others to work to achieve the personal goals and goals of our organization. And it's kind of a cornerstone of management. And the traditional work approach, which is that employees are just resources, assets that need to be worked efficiently. But it is some kind of old, not very human-oriented approach. A more modern approach is a meaningful motivation series based on the identification of the inner identity and needs of employees or teammates that compelling people to act in one way rather than another.

And procedural series of motivations are more than concepts, and they are based primarily on how people behave in light of education and cognition. Alright. Moving a little bit forward. So from planning, organization, motivation to control function of management, The concept of control or verification is a form of administrative activity that goes beyond the concept of control. In addition, it includes the process of the management or management process. Management control is not one time action. It is a continuous process. It includes monitoring and regulating the organization's various activities in order to facilitate the performance of management tasks.

In its most general form, the control process can be defined as the mapping process of achieving the result with planned results. So mapping of planning versus achieved. We have the following management principles: So general principles and private principles. The general principles are the following: applicability, orientation for system work of all parts and some synergistic practices to increase each part of the system to make it into the super system, Multifunctionality of system, the integrity of practices and focus on values. What about specific principles? They are the following: it is an optimal combination of resources, centralization and decentralization in governance. Regarding the context, that could be one or another optimal.

Scientific validity of management practice: measurability, knowledge, and so on. The principle of planning procedures and the principle of combining rights and responsibilities, team weights, some legal aspects and common practices. And what about the subject and object of management? After stages, we can conclude the subject of management and manager is a body or the person who carries out the management action. And regarding the object, it is a separate structure of the organization to which the management action is directed.

The subject is manager and object; it's part of the organizational structure into which action is directed. In the IT field however, the project is a main focus of management. Alright. Dear friends and now coming into project management activities from the general management stages, subject and object of specific project management procedures. By definition, project management is an application of knowledge, skills, tools, and techniques to project tasks to meet the requirements of the project. This definition comes from the project management Body of Knowledge, or PMBOK and determining requirements are also needed.

Also responding to the needs, doubts, and expectations of stakeholders because we're talking about real life projects. Establishing, maintaining, and communicating with stakeholders, stakeholders, management, balancing the competing constraints of the project, content quality, schedule, budget, resources and the risks. These are the questions of real-life scenarios of IT projects. Alright, and dear friends, let's move a little bit further. In the next chapter, we will start with the Waterfall Model. For now, that's it. Thank you for your attention. Keep yourself well. See you soon.

Waterfall Model

Welcome to this chapter regarding the waterfall model. We talked about the waterfall model it is, the classic Cascade model, project management, without unnecessary formality as it is possible to design, debug, and test the software before it is ready for release. In the 70s the cascading model was flawed. And it doesn't matter to the classic coding and bug correction software development. This model emphasizes the original requirements and design, as well as the creation of the communication early in the development process; it means sequential passages and stages which must be completed completely before the next one begins. So the first one completed the stage, and only after the completion the next phase could be implemented.

And product flaws become known only at the end of development as the list of requirements cannot be adjusted at any time. It is a rather rigid model. The concept of making changes is high in such models and we continue to the following details on the waterfall model. There will be some additional things to discuss in this chapter from reminding you of basic stages of waterfall: from requirements to design the implementation and verification of such things, maintenance on the system and in some kind of cascade waterfall. And that's why this model comes into place with such a name. Alright. After that, we're ready for later stages. So in more detail. So collecting and analyzing requirements and it is important to document the requirements for the future software.

Some time should be devoted to discussions of stakeholders over project details. It is also important to take into account all technical limitations that may arise on the customer side. The bottom line of the project and detailed specifications that meet all the requirements of the customer. And other factors that can hamper the development process are the customer deadlines and budget constraints. Each of these things should be mentioned in the requirements. First of all, they should be analyzed and then put in some documents. What about the second stage? And that is software design. It is based on the specification, which includes a description of architecture, design, and basic functions.

Then the software development stage comes into play. At this stage, we include the development of an interactive prototype in the beginning, with little code. As soon as the interactive prototype and design is ready and approved by the customer the development of application standards with lots of lines of code begins. Each model is developed by developers to test this functionality and also non-functional characteristics. It is implemented in a waterfall model on the fourth stage called software testing. After that the fifth stage comes into place and it is software support and maintenance of the project.

Sometimes it is done via dedicated support, sometimes with few specialists who will support the system. And dear friends, there are some benefits of cascading models. Of course, with difficulties it works well for those projects that are sufficiently clear but still difficult to resolve. It's very accessible to understand that the simplest goal is to take the necessary action. So just stages from one, after closing one, second, after closing second one, the third one and so on. It is simple and easy to use as a development process is phased into such direct stages. It is well for stable requirements. If they are stable, it just works most of the time in some percentages.

OK, it is a template in which methods can be put to perform analysis, design, coding, testing and security. So there are plenty of templates and patterns to repeat in this model and it promotes strict control over those project management procedures. If the model is used correctly the facts can be detected early and are not relatively costly. And make it easier for the project manager to plan and set up a development plan, It allows project participants who have completed their phases to participate in other projects. So after they implement this stage, they are free to take action on other projects. This project determines the quality control process, the stages of the model are pretty well defined and understandable for most of the team.

The project process is not hard to trace using basic project management models and timelines, for example Gannt chart. Since the completion of each stage is used as a project stage, the deadlines and time frames could be adopted into such charts. But there are reasonable flaws of such models of cascading waterfall models. Each attempt to go back in one or two phases to fix a problem or flaw, will result in significant increase in costs and failure in the schedule. Because in strict implementation it is impossible But if it is necessary there are no procedures and the processes are very expensive in managerial resources and costs.

And in classic, it is not acceptable at all. This model doesn't show the main software development property to solve the problem. Individual phases are strictly related to certain actions, which differ from the actual work or staff or teams. This model can give the impression of working on a project. It could be, for example, the expression " Thirty-five percent are fulfilled" and it does not make any sense and is not indicated for the project manager because there is no ready feature or something else. We are not sure if this project is working at all, for example. The introduction of all results takes place in the final stages of the model, which also brings some risks.

And this is the source of another risk of the integration stage and quality assurance team when they are coming from component testing into some system tests and there could be no integrity there between the components, for example. There is no procedure on how to solve this because the project is in the final stage and the client hardly familiarizes themself with the system in advance. It happens only at the very end of the life cycle. The user participates in the development process at the beginning and at the end-user acceptance tests. So there is no engagement of customers in the medium of the project, and users can't provide the quality of the product until the entire development process is complete. This is also the source of risks.

Because the needs could evolve and so on. The user does not have the opportunity to gradually get used by the system, The learning process takes place at the end of the cycle when the software is already in operation. This project can be completed and put into line with written requirements, which, however, does not guarantee its launch. So problems that could be solved via an agile manifesto-like "working product is more important than the project documentation" documentation could be written perfectly in such projects, but there could be no working product at all. And risky choices for systems that are unique. Also, some of the drawbacks of such a system. But the list is not yet coming to an end.

There is a need for tight management and control as the model does not provide for the possibility of modifying the requirements. So they were written, they could not be modified. The model is based on documentation's number of documents that can be redundant. There may be problems with this project financing: large amounts of money being distributed, and the model itself is unlikely to fit the redistribution of funds in the process of its implementation. There's no way to take into account rework and interaction outside of product and project development.

As we comprehend, there are some nice things about the waterfall model and it is suitable for large technical projects for the air industry, for example, with each specific should be in order and should be documented well and with some specifics. But for many medium-sized projects, with evolving requirements, it's not suitable for some kind of drawbacks of this model. Thank you for your dedication to comprehending the waterfall model. See you in the following chapter.

Scrum Framework

Dear friends, Welcome back. After discovering the waterfall model we're ready for, delving into another family of methodologies areas, agile methodologies in particular we start with scrum. Scrum is a framework that helps you to solve changing tasks, to deliver products to customers with the best possible value and its definition. And simple to understand, but difficult to perfect mastery. Scrum is a process framework that was started to be used to manage complex products in the early 1990s. Scrum is not a process, technique or exhaustive method, but rather a framework. On the contrary, and it is a framework in which you can use a variety of processes and methods, Scrum makes visible flaws in project management and working methods so that you can continue to improve the product, team and work environment.

And that was the definition of scrum and some activities of scrum. Then we should mention something as a scrum application. And to manage products, we should explore and identify viable markets, technologies, and product opportunities. Develop products and improve them, release products and update them several times a day. Develop and maintain cloud technologies. For example, online, secure, on-demand things and other aspects of cloud things and other environments for product use. Maintain and update products. And these are the areas of context in which project management who implements Scrum will be placed. And after it comes into place, scrum theory.

And Scrum is based on the theory of empirical management, or the so-called concept of empiricism. I.e. The source of knowledge in such a kind of philosophy is experience, And the source of solutions - real data on which decisions are made. So finding some empirical experience, measurement of it, and using real data to improve decisions. And Scrum takes an iterative and incremental approach. And about the iterative, we remember these repeating cycles. And incremental, it is building some features, for example, some working parts of the product to improve predictability and manage the project risks. The process of experiential management is based on the transparency of such procedures and special adaptation.

There are also the following scrum values: Focus on customer needs, commitment of the team to perform well during the sprint and obtain a nice the velocity of creating features, respecting each other all inside the team and outside the team, And openness to new approaches in retrospectives and demos to improve the quality of shipment of products and internal team practices. And one of the team players in Scrum and one of the major figures and rules It is the product owner. Product owner or PO for short, responsible for achieving maximum value for the product. And it is the only person in charge of the managing product backlog, We remember that the product backlog is a shortlist of features that should be implemented.

And product backlog items are described in a clear, understandable way by the product owner. PO manages all of the items in the backlog and tries to best achieve the goals and missions of customers by prioritizing such features. This will optimize the value of work done by the development team and ensure that the product backlog is accessible, transparent and clear to all involved in the process. Using some tools, for example, could be less unfamiliar, for example, JIRA or for such services It could be confluence use or basic tools and product owner guarantees that a development team understands a broader backlog and items are sufficiently shippable for customers.

So is the role of product owner. And we are ready to move a little bit forward. There are some scrum artifacts in such a process. And the product backlog is an ordered list. So defining in more detail, it is not a list of features of a generic list, but some kind of ordered list. So it is a list of known product requirements. And this is the only source of requirements and any necessary changes in the product. So (product backlog is) the source of truth. The product backlog contains data that determines whether changes are needed in the future product releases or not.

Each element of the product backlog must include a description and position number in the backlog and estimate of the required amount of work, Because requirements are constantly changing, the product backlog remains a main artifact. The items at the top of the list are usually better detailed than the items at the bottom because they are faster to implement. They need more details. And in this picture it is kind of the backlog performed in Jira. But any other issue tracking system could be similar. Dear friends, thank you for your dedication to starting or solidifying knowledge in the scrum. See in the following chapter.

Scrum Framework: Backlog, Sprints

Welcome back. And now it's time for continuing the discovery of scrum. Solidify your knowledge of Scrum now. Start this chapter with such things and such and such concepts as sprint backlog. Product backlog - is the ordered number of features and some kind of list of items on the top. It's more detailed. Then we are narrowing it down to the sprint backlog. A subset of the product backlog. A sprint backlog is a backlog of items taken into that current sprint plus a plan to achieve the sprint goal and deliver the product. Now, those three parts, it's an item from the product backlog that will be taken into the sprint by the team. And a plan to achieve a sprint goal. How do they plan to achieve this? And delivering the product and effort is necessary.

The backlog is a development team prediction of what functionality will go in the next increment and what effort is needed to create the working environment. Alright. We're ready to take another step in our journey. This step will be the following after understanding what is the sprint backlog if we are ready to understand the sprint. The sprint concept is a time period of less than a month or four weeks or less, but not less than one week. Which is a shippable product. And if it is incremental, it is usable. Now some kind of feature which has some business value, it is advisable to maintain the duration of the sprint throughout the development process. So if it is chosen for two weeks and that is it. If it is three, then three.

Four, then four. The new sprint starts immediately after the end of the previous one. So no pauses are necessary. The sprint consists of sprint planning. The daily scrum, development procedures, Sprint review, and Sprint retrospectives and it is the so-called Scrum rituals. Alright. And we are ready to increase knowledge in the sprint. And changes that could jeopardize sprint goals are not allowed. So the main task is to reach the goals of the sprint. Product quality should not be reduced. So if it is at some maximum level of quality, it should be kept up as new knowledge becomes available so global work can be refined and rearranged between the product owner and the development team.

So if new knowledge comes into place, some scope could be narrowed or widened the interaction with the product owner. Sprint should be considered a project that lasts no longer than one month. And sprint-like projects are needed to achieve its goals and the maximum duration of the sprint is one calendar month as was mentioned. With longer planning time, goal changes have increased complexity and increased risks are possible. Alright. And for the next step, we are ready and it will be the following: to see the big picture of the sprint. As we know, one picture is worth 1000 words. So from a backlog with some grooming or prioritizing items on the left and then to sprint planning. Some are making some parts of the backlog into the practices.

And then forming its sprint backlog as a subset of the backlog. Then make daily scrums with questions: what was done and what will be done today and what are obstacles. To sprint execution in a given timeframe to create a potentially shippable product increment with a demonstration for customers. Sprint retrospective for internal findings of best and worst practices during the sprint. Dear friends, and in the next chapter we will start with the sprint planning stage for now. Thank you, see you soon.

Scrum: Sprint Planning, Review, Retrospective

Dear friends, after understanding the scrum process as a big picture, we are now ready to deepen our knowledge and not only understand what is the product backlog, what is sprint backlog, what are rituals, but describe them and understand them in more detail. So regarding, Sprint backlog. If a Sprint lasts a month, for example, sprint planning should take no more than eight hours. The scrum team discusses what will be delivered as an increment by the end of the sprint and how the team will achieve that. Only the development team can select the particular items for the product backlog. But it can also get advice from the product owner or other experts. Some advisers could be possible.

But the final decisions are on the team and their decision, which will solidify what will go into the sprint backlog. Since they are committed to doing this, they are responsible for choosing this. And we are ready for the following step. It will be regarded as the next scrum feature, scrum ritual. And it is about daily scrum. Remember this is regarded as three questions, but there are some specifics also. Meeting of the development teams held everybody at the same time during the sprint. And no more than 15 minutes are allowed to these procedures, which the development team plans for work the next 24 hours. The daily scrum increases the likelihood that the development team will reach the sprint end goal.

And the questions that they ask themselves. So we will repeat them once again. What did I do yesterday that helped develop the team to get closer to the sprint goals? What will I do today to help the development team to reach the sprint goal? Do I see any obstacles that can prevent me or the development team from reaching Sprint goals? So they are the major questions in such a situation and in such a ritual.

And we are ready for the following one. And the following one comes into place. And it is a sprint review. After the sprint was completed with each daily ritual. Sprint review comes into place. It is about being conducted at the end of the Sprint. In order to inspect the Increment and adapt a product backlog.

It is done with customers. A scrum team discusses with customers what was done during this sprint. An informal meeting, not very, and formal procedure, it is a kind of demonstration of the product, looking for feedback from customers and further cooperative development. If the Sprint is one month, then the review does not exceed four hours. The results of the sprint reviews is the revised product backlog with some accepted features, with some feedback on them by the end customer. So okay, we're moving a little bit further. And after discussing Daily Scrum and after describing Sprint Review, one more ritual is left for this chapter.

Here is the Sprint retrospective. The sprint retrospective is an opportunity for the scrum team to conduct and inspect on themselves, not on the customer, but on the team as the unit. And it is done to create a plan to improve teamwork in the next sprint. The maximum duration of such a ritual is three hours for a one-month Sprint. Their team members should mention that some cooperation could be performed better between, for example, quality assurance and development teams. New tools could be introduced for business analysis to communicate better inside the team, or more chapters are required to talk with product owners to refine some details. Thank you dear friends for your attention to such things as sprint retrospective, sprint review and daily meetings and see you the following chapters on Scrum methodology. For now, see you.

Scrum: Misc

Dear friends, we have some misc facts which will be nice for you to learn, and they are the following. There is such a role as a product owner in agile. But there is one other specific role for scrum practices. It is SM or Scrum Master. And SM is responsible for the promotion and support of Scrum in accordance with the Scrum Guide. And it is kind of a leader-servant for the scrum team. Scrum Master helps people outside the team to comprehend what is nice and what is useful for their interaction with the scrum team and what is not. Scrum Master helps change these interactions so they can gain maximum value the scrum teams create.

And what is SM doing? It is some kind of role that coaches teams tend to be self-organizing and cross-functional. And the scrum team should be self organized and cross-functional. But there is some kind of coach - the Scrum Master - who can assist the team in doing so. Scrum master also helps create high value products, removes obstacles to team progress. But remember one of the questions on daily stand-up is regarding some obstacles and scrum master's role, which should help the team meet to reduce the negative effects of such obstacles. Scrum master will also facilitate scrum events if necessary. So it could maintain the right form of such events and help to conduct them if necessary. It is some kind of facilitator. Some of the best performers in the scrum activities.

scrum master coaches and the development team in parts of the organizations where Scum is not yet fully understood and accepted. And what about balance in scrum activities? They are the following: It is building the thing and building the thing right. And build it fast. Trying to find a nice spot for these things. To better understand the digital economy of scrum management, it comes into play with graphs such as the Burn-down chart. We see that on Y axes there is effort. Estimating such efforts in playing poker events with some points for difficulties. In iterations, there is some burning down of such points or completing product features.

Within the iteration one there are a number of points and in iteration #2 - 10 points burned down and in iteration three some more and so on. Also iteration #4 and with this number we could measure the team velocity, E.g. it could be 10 points. And work remains for this period and so on. So the burn-down chart is introduced for scrum practice. Dear friends, thank you for being with me on a miscellaneous part of scrum practice. See you in the following chapter on kanban.

Kanban Overview

Dear friends, welcome to the chapter dedicated to Kanban practices. And to increase your understanding of Kanban. Here are some highlights for you. Real-time performance discussion. Full transparency of workflows is presented in Kanban. The stages of work are visually represented on the kanban board. And it is one of the major artifacts in kanban - kanban board. This board allows team members to see the status of the task at any given time. Unlike scrum, the essence of Kanban is to limit the amount of work in progress. I.e. to always work on the same number of tasks or not too many and too few.

For example, not one and not five, six or more (but three on medium). The word kanban consists of two parts and we remember kan means visual, visible. And ban means card or board. So kan for visuals and ban for cards. Diving more to kanban we code to see examples of kanban boards within some issue tracking. For example Jira with such columns as "to do", "In progress", "code review" and for example "done". Some junior generic columns. Kanban board from left to right. So first from the very left edge of the kanban board is a goal column. Here we will find global goals, the big things that we aspire to do, and to adjust our software system to support. Some kind of product backlog.

And the second one - story queue. The next goal contains a queue of stories ready to run. This is the exact queue because the stories in it are ordered at the time of admission. The first story that has come will be started before anyone else. Then the stories are ready to be implemented. So the full product backlog, for example, the stories to implement. But they are prioritized. Then stages of story development. For example, UED - user experience design, business analysis stage, development stage, and quality assurance stage.

And for example, for such purposes could be used custom columns such as: "to do", "In progress", "Resolved", "Uploaded to DEV", "Ready for Demo", "Closed" and "Done". So, dear friends, that was the chapter dedicated to kanban practices. Thank you for your effort in understanding and comprehending Kanban. In the next chapter we will dive into lean practices and to recap on this chapter. See you soon.

Lean and Quiz Preparation

Dear friends, welcome back. To the chapter dedicated to Lean methodology. Lean concepts are regarded with such concepts as defects, production, waiting, non-utilization of talent, extra processing and transportation. There is some association with lean. Now we should define the basics of lean and basic things and the core of lean its value. And that is the basis. So value is a benefit and consumers will gain from using products or services. And lean production regards everything that does not add value to the product losses, which in Japanese, is Muda or waste in English. So the basis of lean production is just the elimination of waste. So gain value and eliminate waste so that is the core principle of lean.

Dear friends, let's focus on learning. And it is reducing losses also, There are a lot of losses in software development. It could be from switching between tasks and losing some attention to implementing unnecessary functions and losing its resources. And focus on learning. The whole process of creating software consists of learning: with each new feature we learn something new. So as in any other engineering activity, we should focus on learning. And also embedded quality. Focus on learning, reducing losses and embedded quality. And what else we should understand about lean.

Later decision making, fast delivery, respect for people, and optimizing the whole system. So starting with optimizing the whole system, we need to optimize the whole system in lean practices, not sub-optimize individual segments. So some system thinking approach. Respect for people. People are the basis of any sort of activity or that software development undoubtedly refers to. We must respect a team by giving them the maximum authority and responsibility for solving technical tasks. And also fast delivery should be implemented. And later decision making. It's very important to make a decision as soon as possible. The most striking example is the creation of the application architecture. For example, Contrary to the big upfront design approach. We only should create architecture for current functionality.

Following the principles of KISS if we are following lean technology, keep it simple and stupid. But stupid at some kind of jargon word. Just give it enough sophistication to meet the required needs. Now let's recap and recapping all this chapter. We will do this recap with some quizzes. Question number one, what is computational thinking? Whether it's fancy notions for counting or a term for the thinking process that happens inside the computer or mental skills of solving complex problems or a mental skill for doing writing activities. So it's not fancy words for counting. What about b a term for the thinking process that happens inside a computer, not maybe some kind of computer knowledge, but not computational thinking. A mental skill that helps solve complex problems. So that is right.

A mental skill to decompose complex problems and other steps. And it is called computational thinking. So question number two. Say if the following steps of solving some programming problem are in the right order. Starting from the problem description. Then identifying important details of the problem, then the decomposition of this problem. Creating an algorithm and evaluating the solution. So it is nice to have a problem description that we should identify important details. It is OK, but it could be a rather huge decomposition. It's nice to have. After we decompose some possible solution to some steps we can create from them some algorithm to combine this path into a single structure and then evaluate our solution.

So that's true. That's OK. Question number three, what do we accomplish by abstracting? A: get rid of all unimportant details, B: transform a work of art into a message. C: break the problem into small sub-parts and D: Confuse people around. No, it's not confusing. It's kind of funny, but no. Break the problem. It could be a funny answer. It could be confusing but it's not so in this quiz. Answer C: break the problem into small subparts. No, it's also not called deconstruction or decomposing. B: transform a work of art into a message. It's nice art, of course, but no, it's not abstract. And get rid of all unimportant details, yeah. Leaving only the important ones form all sorts of details. It is called abstract. So question number four. What's the name of the process that helps to see whether the problem was solved in the most efficient way?

A: evolution, B: pattern recognition, C: decomposition, D: abstraction So, no, it is not abstraction. We figured that in the previous question there is no decomposition. And pattern recognition It is some kind of another engineering technique. So it is an evaluation. Dear friends, you can play with quizzes on interactive assignments on the platform and you can also find some additional questions. And you can solidify your knowledge on this one. For now, thank you for your great effort in the introduction to project management. See you in the following chapters.

Managing Complexity in IT Project Management: Effective Project Delivery

IT projects are notorious for their complexity, with multiple stakeholders, strict constraints, and high risks. However, strong project management can bring order to this complexity, ensuring that technology initiatives are delivered on time, within budget, and to the satisfaction of all stakeholders. This paper explores the evolution of IT project management, the core principles of effective project management, and provides practical tips for managing complexity in IT projects. Keywords: IT project management; Complexity management; Project delivery; Agile methodologies; Waterfall; Gantt charts; Continuous improvement.

IT projects are notorious for their intricate technical details, multiple stakeholder needs, strict constraints, and high risks [1]. These factors can quickly spiral out of control, leading to project delays, cost overruns, and ultimately, failure. However, strong project management can bring order to this complexity, ensuring that technology initiatives are delivered on time, within budget, and to the satisfaction of all stakeholders.

The Evolution of IT Project Management

IT project management has evolved significantly over the past few decades. In the early days of IT, projects were often managed by technical experts who focused primarily on the technical aspects of the project. However, as technology became more complex and projects became larger and more interconnected, the need for a more structured approach to project management arose. In the 1980s and 1990s, project management methodologies such as Waterfall and Gantt charts emerged, providing a framework for managing IT projects. These methodologies focused on breaking down projects into smaller, manageable tasks and creating a linear timeline for project execution.

However, these approaches were limited in their ability to handle complex, dynamic projects. In the 21st century, Agile methodologies emerged as a response to the limitations of traditional project management approaches. Agile emphasizes flexibility, collaboration, and continuous improvement, enabling teams to quickly adapt to changing requirements and deliver high-quality products.

Core Principles of Effective IT Project Management

Effective IT project management is built on several core principles that help manage complexity and ensure successful project delivery. These principles include: Formal Processes: Establishing formal processes and procedures is essential for managing IT projects. These processes provide a structure for project execution, ensuring that all tasks are completed on time and to the required quality standards. Formal processes also help ensure compliance with industry regulations and standards. Systems Thinking: IT projects are part of a larger system, and effective project management requires a systems thinking approach.

This means understanding how the project fits into the broader organizational strategy and how it will impact various stakeholders. Systems thinking enables project managers to identify potential risks and mitigate them proactively. Leadership Skills: Strong leadership is critical for managing complex IT projects. Project managers must possess excellent communication, collaboration, and problem-solving skills to effectively manage teams and stakeholders. They must also be able to motivate and guide team members, provide direction, and make tough decisions when necessary. Stakeholder Management: IT projects involve multiple stakeholders with varying needs and expectations.

Effective stakeholder management is essential for managing these expectations and ensuring that all stakeholders are satisfied with the project outcome. This involves identifying stakeholders, understanding their needs, and communicating effectively with them throughout the project lifecycle. Risk Management: IT projects are inherently risky, and effective project management requires a proactive approach to risk management. This involves identifying potential risks, assessing their likelihood and impact, and implementing mitigation strategies to minimize risk. Team Collaboration: Collaboration is critical for managing complex IT projects.

Project managers must foster a collaborative environment that encourages team members to share ideas, provide feedback, and work together to solve problems. Continuous Improvement: The IT landscape is constantly evolving, and effective project management requires a commitment to continuous improvement. This involves learning from past projects, adopting new technologies and methodologies, and continuously improving processes to enhance project delivery.

Essential Leadership Skills for Project Managers

Project managers play a crucial role in ensuring that projects are delivered on time, within budget, and to the satisfaction of all stakeholders. While technical knowledge is essential for project managers, it is not the only skill required to be successful in this role. Here are some key leadership skills that project managers need to possess: Communication: Effective communication is critical for project managers to collaborate with diverse stakeholders, including team members, sponsors, and clients. They must be able to articulate project goals, progress, and issues clearly and concisely, both verbally and in writing. Organization: Project managers need to be well-organized to juggle multiple tasks and details simultaneously.

They must be able to prioritize tasks, manage resources, and monitor progress to ensure that projects are delivered on time and within budget. Decisiveness: Project managers must be able to make informed decisions quickly, often amidst ambiguity and conflicts. They must be able to weigh the pros and cons of different options, consider the impact on stakeholders, and make decisions that align with project goals and objectives. Accountability: Project managers must be able to hold themselves and their team members accountable for their actions and results. They must be able to balance accountability with flexibility, knowing when to intervene and when to allow team members to take ownership of their work.

Strategic focus: Project managers must be able to maintain a strategic focus on business objectives, ensuring that projects align with the organization's overall strategy and goals. They must be able to prioritize tasks and resources accordingly, ensuring that projects deliver the desired outcomes. Team motivation: Project managers must be able to motivate their team members to perform at their best. They must be able to empower team members, provide guidance and support, and recognize and reward outstanding performance. Stakeholder engagement: Project managers must be able to engage and manage stakeholders effectively, ensuring that their needs and expectations are met throughout the project lifecycle.

They must be able to communicate project progress, issues, and risks to stakeholders in a timely and transparent manner. Commitment to continual learning and improvement: Project managers must be committed to continual learning and improvement, recognizing that project management is a constantly evolving field. They must be willing to update their skills and knowledge to stay current with industry trends and best practices. By blending hard skills and soft skills, project managers can deliver results in dynamic, high-pressure environments. They must be able to lead and motivate their teams, manage stakeholders, and make informed decisions that align with project goals and objectives.

With the right leadership skills, project managers can ensure that their projects are delivered on time, within budget, and to the satisfaction of all stakeholders. Some Examples Several examples illustrate the power of effective IT project management in action. One such example could be the rollout of a new customer relationship management (CRM) system for a large enterprise. The project could involve multiple stakeholders, complex data migrations, and integration with existing systems. By applying formal processes, systems thinking, and leadership skills, the project manager was able to deliver the project on time and within budget, resulting in significant improvements in customer engagement and sales productivity.

Another example is the development of a mobile application for a healthcare provider. The project could require collaboration between technical teams, clinicians, and patients to create an application that met the needs of all stakeholders. The Benefits of Disciplined Project Management Project management is a critical component of any organization's success, particularly in today's fast-paced and rapidly changing technological landscape. When done correctly, project management can deliver a wide range of benefits that help organizations achieve their goals and objectives.

Here are some of the key advantages of disciplined project management: Increased likelihood of finishing on time and within budget: By establishing clear timelines, milestones, and budgets, project management helps ensure that projects are completed on schedule and within financial constraints. This helps organizations avoid costly delays and scope creep, ultimately saving time and resources. Higher quality through defined requirements and standards: Project management involves defining clear requirements and standards for projects, which helps ensure that the final product meets the needs of stakeholders and customers. This leads to higher quality outputs and greater customer satisfaction.

Better risk protection through proactive planning: Project management involves identifying and mitigating risks that could impact the project. By developing contingency plans and risk management strategies, organizations can minimize the impact of unexpected events and ensure that projects stay on track. Greater visibility into status through monitoring: Project management involves regular monitoring and reporting of project progress. This provides stakeholders with greater visibility into the status of projects, enabling them to make informed decisions and take corrective action if needed.

More accountability through formal change control: Project management involves establishing formal change control processes to ensure that changes to the project are properly documented, approved, and implemented. This promotes accountability and helps prevent unauthorized changes that could impact the project's success. Optimized resource allocation and less waste: Project management helps organizations optimize resource allocation and eliminate waste. By identifying and eliminating inefficiencies, organizations can streamline processes, reduce costs, and improve productivity.

Higher stakeholder satisfaction and smoother adoption: Project management involves engaging stakeholders throughout the project lifecycle, ensuring that their needs are met and that they are satisfied with the final product. This leads to greater adoption and usage of the project's outputs, ultimately benefiting the organization. The Importance of IT Project Management IT projects are critical to business success, and effective project management is essential for delivering these projects on time, within budget, and to the satisfaction of all stakeholders.

Here are some reasons why IT project management is important: Aligns IT with Business Objectives: IT projects are initiated to support business objectives, and effective project management ensures that these objectives are met. By aligning IT projects with business objectives, organizations can achieve strategic goals and improve overall performance [2]. Reduces Risk: IT projects are inherently risky, and effective project management identifies and mitigates these risks. By having a structured approach to project management, organizations can minimize the likelihood of project failures and reduce the impact of any issues that do arise [3]. Improves Efficiency: IT project management helps organizations streamline their processes and improve efficiency.

By having a clear understanding of project scope, timelines, and resources, organizations can optimize their use of resources and deliver projects more quickly and effectively. Enhances Collaboration: IT projects involve multiple stakeholders, and effective project management enhances collaboration among these stakeholders. By fostering collaboration and communication, organizations can ensure that all stakeholders are aligned and working towards the same goals. Improves Quality: IT project management focuses on delivering high-quality products that meet the needs of stakeholders.

By having a structured approach to project management, organizations can ensure that their products are of high quality and meet the requirements of stakeholders. Optimizes Resource Utilization: IT project management helps organizations optimize their use of resources. By having a clear understanding of project scope, timelines, and resources, organizations can allocate resources effectively and avoid wastage. Improves Customer Satisfaction: IT projects are often initiated to improve customer satisfaction, and effective project management ensures that these projects deliver the expected outcomes.

By focusing on customer needs and expectations, organizations can improve customer satisfaction and build loyalty. Supports Innovation: IT project management supports innovation by enabling organizations to deliver new products and services quickly and effectively. By fostering a culture of innovation and experimentation, organizations can stay ahead of the competition and achieve strategic goals. Enhances Reputation: Effective IT project management enhances an organization's reputation by delivering high-quality products and services that meet the needs of stakeholders. By consistently delivering successful projects, organizations can build a reputation for excellence and attract new customers.

Supports Business Growth: IT projects are often initiated to support business growth, and effective project management ensures that these projects deliver the expected outcomes. By focusing on business growth and strategic objectives, organizations can use IT projects to drive growth and expansion. Disciplined project management is essential for organizations that want to achieve their goals and maximize returns on IT initiatives. By delivering projects on time, within budget, and with high quality, project management helps organizations stay competitive and achieve success in today's fast-paced technological landscape.

Effective IT project management is essential for delivering technology initiatives that meet the needs of stakeholders and ensure the success of organizations. By adopting the core principles of formal processes, systems thinking, leadership skills, stakeholder management, risk management, team collaboration, and continuous improvement, project managers can effectively manage complexity and ensure successful project delivery.

By following the guidance provided in this paper, project managers can deliver high-quality IT projects that meet the needs of stakeholders and drive business success. References Project Management Institute. (2013). A guide to the project management body of knowledge (PMBOK guide). Project Management Institute, Inc. Agile Manifesto. (2001). Agile manifesto. Agile Alliance. Kitson, S. (2019).

Business Culture

Hello there. I help businesses, leaders that people think in 3D. And I work around the world speaking, training, consulting and helping people do this. I've written a book all about what we call 3D businesses. They are dramatically and demonstrably different from their competitors about this Book. Well, the challenges facing business leaders today have never been bigger. We're in a fast moving, ever changing world. There's increasing employee expectations and rising staff turnover levels in lots and lots of sectors. People are finding it difficult to find, attract and retain quality people. This is all exacerbated by what we call a CCTV world, a world of never ending change, ever increasing connectivity, greater and greater transparency.

And it's all happening with such velocity. It all makes things much more difficult for today's business leaders. And a different approach is needed, a dramatically and demonstrably different approach. Even we call it 3D leadership. And what you're going to learn in this Book is what is culture and why? It's a deciding factor in staff recruitment and retention. In today's business world, it is influencing your culture both positively and negatively and what you can do about it. How 3D leaders create, embed and reinforce a culture that engages, empowers and enables their people and creates real competitive advantage. The key steps to help you do it, too. We're going to explore some of the key ingredients of winning culture, cultures and how you can make them work for you and ensure that everyone your business behaves in the way you want them to.

We'll explore how to establish and develop effective systems and processes to report, to support and reinforce this. How to establish a culture that helps attract and retain quality people. How to develop reward and recognition systems that work and will provide proven practical strategies and tactics to improve your culture using real examples of businesses and their leaders who've made this sort of work and hopefully help you do that, too. Practical tools and techniques get ready on board and how to develop your own OBOR culture improvement plan to make this work for you. So by the end of this Book, you'll know how to identify the things that are influencing your culture positively or negatively.

And what you need to do about them. Understand the principles of our uber culture model, how to use them to create the culture you want in your business. Get everybody on board to establish a culture that differentiates you, creates real competitive advantage, and evaluates all the practical options to improve your culture in your organization. You'll use the uber culture model to make a real difference, make a real impact, and help you develop a clear plan of attack to make it all work. Do we know academic theories or magical answers? But you'll get real examples of people who've done it and are doing it. Practical techniques you catch developing, using your role in your business. And we'll provide you with toolkits and templates you can download and use to help you make all this work. So let's get started.

What Exactly Is Culture And Why Bother?

What exactly is culture? I'll tell you a story, I was us winning a training program and I was talking about first direct bank, and we often talk about them. I think they're a great example of a dramatic demonstration from business. And there's a guy on the program telling me about his girlfriend who worked at first, DiREKT, and he said she's completely obsessed about working there. In fact, the other week she was in the queue in a supermarket. She always looked to see what credit card people were using to pay for their shopping, sort of if they're using a first direct one. There was a guy in front of her and you got his first direct card out and started to pay. And it wouldn't work. It wouldn't work. Keep pressing it. Oh, he's all flustered.

Anyway, she said, I'll sort that out. And she actually paid his bill of twenty one pound thirty four people. You know what we're doing? It's all right. Just give me the details. I've got your card details here. We'll sort it out on Monday. I said seriously, yep. On the Monday she came in to work on her desk was a bouquet of flowers. This guy had run up to the bank, told her the amazing thing this lady had done. Her boss had actually given a big bouquet of flowers and put 50 pounds into her account to actually count the money that she'd actually spent. That is what culture is all about. Would people in your business do anything like that? I suspect most of us wouldn't. And it's a fairly extraordinary story.

But I'm trying to sort of show you here that culture is one of things that can make a real big difference. So what exactly is culture? Well, before I came along for this to run this this Book, I got my old MBA notes out and I discovered that culture is a pattern of shared basic assumptions that the group learned as it solves its problems of external adoption and internal integration that has worked well enough to be considered valid and therefore to be taught to new members of the correct way to perceive, think and feel in relation to all those problems. I've no idea what that means. So the definition that I like to use, and this is one of the things we use with our clients, is it's the way we do things around here positively or negatively, consciously or unconsciously. Your culture is the way you do things around here.

A lovely example of culture that I also like. I call Herb Keller, who sets up Southwest Airlines there, a cheap and cheerful in the states, very, very successful and the like, Ryanair. But they smile. And one of the things that day he actually described culture as being is what people do when no one's looking. So one of the things I'm going to explore is exactly what does your culture look and feel like? I was swearing in a seminar that all about culture was a competitive advantage. And this managing director of a manufacturing business came up to me after saying this and this is fascinating, this stuff, he ran a business just outside Barnsley in South Yorkshire, and he said, I'm fascinated with this because we haven't got a culture of our place.

And I said, you have. He said, we have nothing. I'm telling you, if I came to your business, I would get a feel for your culture. We haven't got one. I said, you have said we haven't. Nobody gives a—to our place. That's your culture. Your culture is the way you do things around here, both positively, negatively. But it also is fair to say when you're there and when you're not, is often seen as a soft, touchy, feely side of a business. But my experience suggests it's actually the hardest. Why? Well, because it deals with attitudes and behaviors, which all seem a bit vague and can be hard to manage. It's much easier to talk about territories, product life cycles, tout sales targets, margins and advertising budgets because they're real and tangible.

In fact, in reality, culture is very tangible. As customers, we often experience the culture of business simply by talking to and interacting with employees, whether it's by email, by telephone. Ever walked into a business, into an office, into a factory, into a company, into a shop? This doesn't feel right. It's often the culture in winning businesses. Culture is an integral part of their competitive vantage. It's not left to choice and left not to chance. They actually work on it to make it work for them. So why is culture so important? Well, the Deloitte Global Capital Human Trends report suggests 94 percent of executives, 88 percent of employees believe a distinct workplace culture is important to business success. Well, that's nice. The Center for Workforce Report suggests that culture and employee engagement are the number one issue for the world's business leaders.

They also said that 79 percent of employees say recognition tied to core values gave them a stronger sense of company goals and objectives. In other words, the values drive what's expected. According to the Glassdoor report 2020, 56 percent of workers ranked a strong workplace culture as more important than salary. Sixty six percent said their organization's culture was one of the main reasons for staying in their job. Creating the right culture can be a great way for retaining people, recruiting them in the first place, and maximizing their performance to actually create great customer experiences. Well, this isn't a soft and touchy feely thing. It's a thing that can differentiate your business and make you stand out in the crowd to both your customers and potential employees.

What Influences Your Culture?

What are the things that influence your culture? Well, there are lots of things, and what I'm going to do is take you through a list of them. They start looking at this, but as ever, download a tool kit to help you assess yourself and your business against these things. Because all these things in your organization do one of two things. They act positively or negatively. So going to go through them and just see what this actually looks like for you and for your organization. So, number one, influencer, your working environment. The very fact that your office that you're in will actually have an impact on how people behave, whether it's neat, tidy, whether it's and I'll stress again, as somebody who won Sheffield's Messy Desk of the Year competition a number of years ago, I actually would argue that I find it be more creative in a messy environment.

What I'm saying here is the working environment you've got will shape your culture positively or negatively to your organizational history, where the organization and where the business has come from. A fresh faced new business dynamic they start to look at by young entrepreneurs is probably, I suspect, going to have a different culture to a well-established manufacturing business going down three generations. I want to stress not necessarily right or wrong. I've seen some very, very well-run, traditional, inverted commas, organizational businesses that can still attract the right people and still grow and develop and adapt as they need to do these things. In fact, one of the things for me when I see some organizations is that they are held back by the history of the business.

Others use it to drive and shape things forward. So think about your organizational history, your marketplace, the marketplace you're in will influence the culture. Again, a small engineering business in the

Northeast, I suspect, will have a different culture to a dynamic, fast growing Silicon Valley business and dealing with it and those sorts of things. What I'm saying here is not right or wrong, but it will actually influence your culture, your employees, their background, their expertise, their knowledge. But a key thing on this one for me, one of the things we see in lots and lots of businesses is that some businesses, because they recruit people in their own likeness and in the same way they become the same old, same old, same old.

They don't grow and develop. So I'm not saying here you've got to have lots of clones. In fact, I would argue what the best businesses do is actually embrace and support and encourage diversity. It's not necessarily can people be the same as you, is can they enhance and add value to your culture? Your systems and processes will shape and reinforce the culture of your organization. Computer says no. It's just a classic example. I see lots of businesses where the culture is completely driven by systems. As long as you fill that form and you're going to be OK, it actually doesn't help people move forward and drive things forward. Number six, your policies that will be written, policies in your business.

But I think it's worth pointing out there will also be some unwritten ones. There will be things that people quote in your organization verbatim and they will see written down anywhere. And these unwritten rules, some can be positive, but some can be negative. What do your policies do? They reinforce the culture you want or do they actually hold you back? Seven Your customs and rituals from. We've always done it this way and we always have a meeting on a Tuesday morning. Well, this is how we deal with new employees. Are they positive ones or are they negative ones? Customs and rituals can be a very, very powerful way of actually moving your organization forward. They can also be the thing that can hold them back.

Eight signs and symbols. I visited a business called Web Mart, run by Geico Simon Bill Cliff. He runs his business on capitalist Marxist principles. It makes a lot of profit and he shares it. And you can imagine it's quite a unique culture in that organization. But I turned up at their organization, their Bicester head office walked in, and I was greeted by the receptionist who gave me a cup of coffee just as I liked it. But by the side of the reception area was a sign that said, do you need a recharge? And next to that were a number of sockets for different phones to actually allow you to just plug your phone in and get it charged while you're with them. It's not going to change the world, but a little thing that just shows that customers are important.

I also once went to a restaurant. I went upstairs to the restaurant, nipped to the loo by mistake, walked into the staff room and on the whiteboard Saturday evening, there was a student on the whiteboard. There was a note from I guess the managing director said, well done, guys, wish we smashed those targets this week and shafted the customers. Let's see if we can get some more next week. Now, I know I was supposed to see that, but I'm not sure that we should be talking about shifting customers. If those are the things that people see, then maybe that's how people act. Just to let you know, that business went bust about 18 months later, so maybe said something about them. Nine of your war stories.

What do people talk about from the past? Good or bad things that reinforce what we do and how we do. It could be great stories of customer service or equally it could be things like so-and-so wouldn't. Let you do that. She once worked with an organization. Well, I spent a bit of time. The mayor asked me to spend some time in the company, going to see what's going on and report back. I actually said that I think you've got a real problem with that with Richard. What do you mean? I said, well, a number of people hear me saying that hearsay or Richard would let you do that, which he says you can't do.

We actually heard some people quoting who never even met him. What we see in the best businesses they do is they create positive war stories and reinforce and champion their champions. Are you creating war stories now that actually reinforce and shape the behaviors you want 10 your goals and targets? By definition, a business looking to treble in size, I suspect will have a different culture to an organization Kwapis, where it is not right or wrong 11. What do you measure both formally and informally, what are the things that you put a lot of emphasis on? Because of my experience of this, if you tell people that the only thing that matters is sales through the door, then that's what people focus on.

In other words, what we see in the best businesses is that they actually measure and recognize key things like behaviors, how they want people to behave, as well as hitting the goals and targets. 12. What you reward both formally and informally. I don't know if you know, for example, in 1862, but if a history chapter for you here. A hundred and sixty five thousand convicts were sent to Australia by boat, less than 50 percent survived. Edwin Chadwick, who was a lawyer and a civil servant, looked at this and said, this can't be right. It turns out that the ship's captains and the ship's owners were actually rewarded for a number of people who could get on the boats. So guess what? They ran them full.

He actually said to the government, you've got to change this. We will now only start rewarding the people who are taking these over to Australia by those that survive. Survival rates went up to ninety eight point five percent. I'm not suggesting that's something you're going to start doing in your business. What I'm trying to get you to think about here. What are you rewarding and recognizing? A great story of a Swedish village, but a thorough, fair road coming through quite quickly. People generally beat the speed limit as they go through it. So they came up with a town council, with a little scheme. And basically, as you drove into the village, if you were below the 50 kilometers an hour sign, vehicle recognition spotted your car and it said, congratulations, you've just won a ticket for the speed draw.

If you go over 50 kilometers an hour, congratulations. You've just been fined and you've donated to the prize for the speed draw. And the words those that were going over the speed limit will find there was going under it, we're actually rewarded. Guess what? They showed that speed limits dropped magnificently as I went through these things. So what are you rewarding? But what are you also tolerating? Thirteen. The leaders. According to Mercer H.R. report, only 45 percent of UK employees feel that their managers behave in a way which is consistent with their company values. In other words, they can say all this great stuff. Put it up on the website. Put it on the posters.

Do they actually live it? Just to give you an example of what this really looks like in the real world. I mentioned the MDY from the company who told me that culture was that they wanted to go to our place and to be used to having a word with my lot because they don't listen to me. So I want you to come up and do a bit of training and we'll get them all sorted. I said, well, I'll come up. I've just come to explore and see what's going on. So I went up to his business and it was a small little manufacturing business on the side of the money manufacturing. I was a little shed when the sad reception spelt wrong. Anyway, I walked into the reception area, pressed this buzzer, and his voice went, Hello. I said, I'm here to see Mr. Smith. I'm trying to sell him something.

I went, No, no, I'm a customer. " I'm just waiting, OK. Wait there. And I sat down in this little room that had got a coffee table with three brown plastic coffee cups still on it with cigarette stubs in. There was a six week copy of The Daily Mirror, a six week old copy that I remember that well, some industry journals on the wall, two, three or four years old. And I sat there for 17 and a half minutes. Five different people walked past me. Not one person said, Can I help you? Are you OK?

If this guy comes out, he's a lovely chap on them. So, so I've been told. Right. Come on, you can have a real deal with this law. I'm always telling him, I said, can I just ask, what are you telling them? I'm telling them customers are really important and it's vital we look after them.

I said, could I just ask, do you walk through there every day? He said, yeah. I said, what do you think you are telling your team if you think that's acceptable? So this is not about putting up. It's actually about living this stuff and doing these things. So we've gone through these factors. What I encourage you to do is download that talk, if not done it, or have a look at the one you've got and actually work through it and work out which of these things are acting positively or negatively to support or detract from the culture you actually want. Consider getting other people involved in this. Let them have a look at it and work out what's happening in your business and what you need to do to move things forward. It's a great culture.

What's Your Culture?

What is your culture? What I would like you to do is just jot down a few words, phrases. Don't worry about a mission statement and document. I'm just looking to just jot it down now. I'll think out loud. What are the words and phrases that describe your culture? The good, the bad and the ugly. Just jot those things down and then have done that. Just think a bit about what aspects of it you are happy about? What are the things you're not so happy about? But also ask you to think about this. How do you know that's your culture? How clear a picture do you actually have? You never know. And this is what are some things I see in some organizations. Things change when senior people are around. Not necessarily for the better.

And what I encourage you to think about here is try and create a clear picture of what your culture is. One of the best ways of doing that is to give your people a—good listening, to ask everybody in all areas and all departments at all levels. And here are some questions I would encourage you to consider. Question one: How would you describe our culture in just three words? Question two, What would you tell a friend about working here? Question three, What one thing should we change? Because you, for one thing, should never change one thing, should we never stop doing? Question five, what do we reward and recognize around here? Both formally and informally. I mean, couldn't you just get people to work on those questions formally or informally, start having those conversations, get as many opinions as you can.

So, I mean, again, it's quite powerful if you look at question one. Please describe our culture in just three words. I would encourage you to go to his Wordle dot org and actually type in the word because it was typing the words. The more a word is used, the bigger it page on the image that comes up. And it's a very, very wonderful way of visually painting a picture of what your culture actually is, having created this picture. Create some time now to think a bit about which aspects of your culture are you happy with. Not so happy with it, but also investigate all their differences in different regions and different offices in different departments, different hierarchies. Can you actually work out what this means for you? In other words, your turn to create this picture of where you are now? You've then got something to build on as we move on to looking at how we can create an uber culture in your organization. That's the next chapter.

The Principles Of UBER Culture

3D businesses create an uber culture. You beat. And I'm going to explain what it is about, and then for the rest of the Book, we're going to take you through the different elements of this and work out what they mean for you and for your organization. So the view is that everybody understands what's expected of them and behaves accordingly and consistently to people. It's spelt out to people how we want them to behave. The B is that systems and processes are built to support and reinforce the culture and the behaviors you want. People are engaged, empowered and enabled to deliver. That's the E and the R is that people are rewarded and recognized for doing so. So Uber understands how to build systems.

People engaged, empowered, enabled, are rewarded and recognized for doing it. OK, we're not going to make this stuff quite tangible. And what I'd like to do is think about how your business measures up. So download the assessment toolkit. And what this does, it takes you through a series of statements, helps you identify where in those four areas you are doing well and not so well. And again, I would really encourage you to get others to do it, too. That helps you work out what it is you need to do.

Value Your Values

3D leaders value their values and create a culture that creates a competitive antigen. And it's all about behaviors. They spell them out. And that's what it's all about. It's not about posters. It's not about just telling everybody the usual stuff. I'm yet to walk into an organization, say, oh, yeah, and our culture values. You'll see it at the reception there. We don't care about our customers that exploit our stuff. We'll put wonderful posts up there. And I'm not saying we shouldn't. But the key here is do we actually use them to shape the behaviors we actually want? And this thing starts with you. 3D leaders value their values.

What exactly are values? Well, my experience suggests that they are the things that you stand for. The things you believe in. It's the way you work, the things that influence your decisions. What you do, how you do it, and the things that define and differentiate you, your personal core values, define who you are. And a company's core values ultimately define the company's character and brand for an individual's character, his destiny. For organizations, culture is destiny. That's a quote from a wonderful guy called Tony Shea, who built a business called Zappos on 10 core values. Now, that site might sound very touchy feely.

2009, he actually built the business and sold it to Amazon for one point two billion dollars was quite interesting. Is part of the deal Amazon allowed to go nowhere near them? They leave them to run their business on these 10 core values. It's very lucky to visit them a couple of years ago. And I can tell you now they really live this stuff. So what's the value of values? Well, again, my experience suggests that they can do a number of key things. And this hopefully will help you understand maybe why we should be doing these things. Your values can help define the fundamental character of your business. They can shape how we do things around here. They can create a sense of identity and help build the brand and the reputation of the business. They can determine how resources will be allocated.

They can reduce game playing politics and confusion and provide guidance for acceptable, unacceptable behaviors. They can also help recruit and retain the right people. However, I will stress the word can is key because it all seems very, very easy on paper and it's not on paper. That's the point. Yes, you can write these things down. What this is about is developing something that actually shapes what you do and how you do it. So simply producing a set of values is not the answer. You've actually got to do something with them. So therefore, please, please, please don't get to step one. Just develop the values and do nothing else and maybe hear some words of warning to maybe help you shape this and make it work for you.

Because here are seven common mistakes I see businesses make when they look to establish their values. Mistake one, they pay lip service to it. Many leaders think once they've ticked the box of establishing their values, they can actually leave it at that. I hear so many directors and. Oh, yes, and I've got a set of core values. And what are they? So think about delighting customers and empowering people. You see it on the reception desk as you go down there. They're just paying lip service to it. There's no meaning to it. And even worse, their actions actually contradict what they say. So those lovely posters are there. But actually, nobody's living it. I was once working with an organization, and one of their core values was that we empower and engage our people to maximize their performance.

And I was talking to a number of employees about what was going on. And this one particular guy, Schultz, lost it all. So. Right. Waste of time. So what do you mean he goes? Well, I was asked. I asked what sort of training Book I want to take at a local college to help me develop my I.T. skills. So I went to my line manager. I'm going to go on this.

They said we can't afford to send you on holiday on Books. So you don't know it's free. Yeah. He says, OK, I'll let you start having half a day off. No, no. It's in the evening. Books in the evening. But because it starts at half past five, I need to leave half an hour early to go to the Book. Well, OK, I'll let you start doing that. No, it's OK. I'll work my lunch hour so I can do that so I can do it. Well, if you start doing that, all start doing it, he said.

But what about that post that says we value our people and want to maximize their potential and their performance. They. That's the sort of Bush and these are paid to do. In other words, they've got these posters, but nobody's doing anything with them. Mistake number two is there are too many. It's basically a list of things put together that don't really define how you want things to be. It's a catchall approach. So it really dilutes things. And the result is that they become meaningless or sometimes even contradictory. So maybe identify a core set of values. Mistake number three. Is there somebody else's someone in another organization's values or we'll have those two? They actually believe.

But by taking those vials of a successful organization, they'll be like them or even worse than being a management consultant to provide them. I'm not saying management consultants can't help shape them. So what do I do? But let's be honest. Zappos is Zappos pinching their Temko values isn't going to work in your business. That's not to say that you can't learn from them when it comes to making this stuff work. And there is a toolkit. You can download an ebook with 40 chapters from Zappos that I learned. We went to visit them. So have a look at that. But please, please, please do not try to nick their values. Mistake them for them off the shelf.

So even worse, they just pick out some nice common sense words and phrases that don't really shape what's going on. And they certainly don't establish the things that maybe are unique about your business.

So my experience suggests in lots of cases, lots of businesses use the same old words and phrases as everybody else. So. There's nothing that differentiates helps you stand out, so there's nothing that actually means that you are unique as a business. Booz Allen Hamilton, an Aspen Institute Business Society program researcher, said that they actually found that most organizations' values include similar words and ideas.

Ninety percent of them talk about ethical behavior or integrity. 88 percent mentioned commitment to customers. Seventy six percent say teamwork and trust. Now, I want to stress there's nothing wrong with those words, per se. But let's be honest, they're just the same as in some cases, they're what people should be doing anyway. Mistake number five. And this is what I think. Again, I see people do it. The focus is on making a nice word that looks good on a poster. They start and get creative and make sure that the values that create a nice word that when they read them are nice in a row. An example of a business I saw where they cope with their core values and the values they said were good quality. And they've taken the G from the good, good quality.

They talked about building the relationships that were in R the E of exceeding expectations. The aim of action came out there to take action. And it's all about working as a team, the T. So guess what? It was great. But it felt so forced. He didn't really have the credibility. People could almost see that they were just tagging words on to make it look good. So the first go into actually making a nice word, rather, that is spelling out how we want things to be. Mistake number six is that the meaning is missing. We're back to the idea of lots of wonderful words and phrases, but people don't really understand what they mean for them in their day-to -day lives. Again, it often resorts to some of the things above. But a key reason is that they don't actually shape behaviors because the behaviors themselves are not spelt out. In other words, the value statements are open to interpretation.

My idea of common sense, my idea of teamwork might be different to yours. And mistake number seven. Is there not a leadership thing? What I mean by that is that they're not lived and driven by the leaders. 3-D businesses and 3-D leaders live and breathe their values. And this is a set that's driven by the leaders. And that doesn't mean they're the only ones doing it, but they do actually reflect their passion, their personal drivers and the things they value, the things that they think are important and the things that they say they will not back on. They will not actually put away and actually not use in their business. But what we sometimes see is that they don't involve and engage with us in doing it. And what I'm seeing in 3-D business is, yes, it's led by those at the top, but they engage those people, they involve them.

In fact, the best leaders do invite people to get involved in shaping the behaviors they want. It's not about designing them by committee, and it's definitely not binding them to H.R. or even worse as management consultants. But it's about taking responsibility and making them work for you. We've actually put together a fun quiz to help you see what values look like. Download the quiz. You actually see ten sets of company values from different businesses around the world with some potential answers. Your challenge is to see if you can work out whose is whose. Please don't use them just to copy them. What? I'm just going to show you what this looks like in the real world. So you can get a real feel for it. So you can maybe start shaping up your values. So how can you establish your values? Well, first of all, do not copy this. What's the next chapter to find out how and how you can make it work for you?

How To Establish Your Values

So how can you establish your values? Well, there are three basic steps to doing it. I'm going to take you through these three steps and actually work out how you can make them work for you. And this is the key bit. Please, please, please do not do this by rote. Are you going to work out what this means for you? Step one is to establish them. Work out what they are, what they mean for you. Step two is about making them meaningful. And step three is them living them. And that's the difficult bit. So let's look at step one. And it's about establishing your core values or maybe reviewing your existing ones. It may be that you've got some core values. You've got some in your organization, in your business. Very often when I go into companies, I mean, oh, you've got a set of core values.

What are they? Uh, what I'm suggesting here is that maybe they're not actually therefore driving what's going on. So block some time out and don't do it today because you're busy doing this. Give yourself some breathing space. Consider involving us. And quite a bit of time to work out what you're going to do to define how you want things to be around him. If you have got some existing values, then review them some questions to consider. Are they meaningful? Are they relevant? And have they lived? Find out what others think. I worked with an organization where I did a seminar on this stuff when the end came to town, and they have suddenly realized that I don't think cars are relevant and lived and meaningful.

So we did some workshops with some of their guys and got their thoughts and views on some of the people who said, I've no idea what it means. It's there, but we don't understand it. So we reshape them. They didn't have to change the whole ethos of what they're trying to do. It was the wording that they actually changed so that people could understand what they actually meant. Most people hadn't done a PhD in management thinking burned to understand what this guy's vision and values actually were. So find out what others think. Get their views and opinions and consider involving them in the process. And then your goal is to establish a set of values that define how you want things to be around here. And again, start off with I would encourage you just to use some of these questions.

You'll see them in the template that you can download to actually explain how to go about working on this. But here are some questions to consider. What's important to me, to us in terms of how we do business. What beliefs and principles shape our decisions or my decisions? What would I do? We never compromise. What do we do that differentiates our business? What do we dislike about how other businesses do things and what will we never do? What behaviors should I demonstrate in everything that we do? And what I'm suggesting here is write lots down. Just don't worry about the words we think. Just get lots of stuff done there.

Put it on Post-it notes. Use these questions to just create the words and phrases that work for you. Just get them done. Please feel free to involve other people. If he's a leader, I would encourage you to think about this. This is not about compromising your core beliefs. So you manage to shape it, but get them all together. Once you've done that, group them together, which is why Post-it notes work quite well, because you suddenly start to see some things overlap. Once you've written everything down, look for groups of words or phrases that can be linked together. Don't be afraid to add words and phrases and be prompted by what you see equally. Feel free to delete any words and phrases that you've put up there. You don't have to use them because you've put them down.

When you start to look at it, you actually think that's normally what I'm about. But your challenge is to shape up your core values, focus on the ones that you really believe in, the ones that drive you the value up and differentiate you and use words and phrases that mean things to you and your business. So what I'm suggesting again here, don't think about what might go on a website. Work out what works for you internally. Don't just generate words that anybody else is using. Find out what it means to be in your business. Make sure they reflect how you want your business to be. So what I'm suggesting you do here is establish a core set of values, words and phrases that mean something to you that you believe in one or two percent. And please ensure they are authentic, specific and real.

And just to show you how this works in the real world, an organization I worked with in Rotherham. I'll get to all the best places within hospice. It is a charity, does an amazing job caring for people who have cancer and have been doing so for 20 years. And one of the things that we did, we actually looked at reshaping their core values. We've had a set of values that have been published many years ago. And what I did was I worked with the senior team to help shape them. But what we did, we engaged employees from all different parts of the organization. We did staff surveys. We did discussion groups. We got their thoughts and ideas on whether they actually felt the existing values we understood relevant, used and lived.

And we got some mixed messages. So what we then did as a team using the inputs, all the people came up with their core values and we could reshape them. Some of them were the same as before, but we reshaped them. And their core values are caring, working together, trust, respect, and inspiration. I'm not saying those should be your values. Your challenge is to work out what this looks like for you. So download the toolkit to help you shape up or reshape your core values. And then once you've done that, your challenge is to work out how do we make them meaningful? And this is all about spelling out the behaviors you want to actually make this stuff work. So what's the next chapter? To help you do that?

Create The Behaviors You Want

I mentioned in previous chapters that sometimes people publish values that don't mean anything. And the danger is that people also interpret them differently. So they actually interpret things as they see fit. So what we're suggesting here is step one was to actually create your values. Step two is to make them meaningful. And that means turning them into behaviors. How can you do that? Well, one of the ways you look at it is this. If someone was living this value, what would they be doing? Reed Hastings, the founder of Netflix, he talks about real company values are the behaviors and skills that we particularly value in fellow employees.

Now, what we see 3-D businesses and 3D leaders do is they turn their values into tangible behaviors, establish the things that people will be doing if they will live in these values in the day to day, translate them into meaningful behaviors that people would see or experience and ensure that they are proactive and positive statements. So some things to avoid generalizations such as is nice because your definition of nice might be very different to mine. So be specific and allow you to actually assess whether people are consistently doing this. Occasionally doing this. Rarely doing this. Never doing this. If a statement is done in a proactive way, you can actually start to use this to shape and influence how people are doing things.

And the other thing for me is to think about if these are the behaviors meaningful to the people you want to actually use them? So I said again, if you've got people from different educational levels, different departments, different regions, make sure the language you use is in a way that works for them. Netflix has nine core values. I'll take your calls very quickly. Judgment, communication, impact, curiosity, innovation, courage, passion, honesty, selflessness on their own. They probably don't mean much. And you could argue that only businesses, what they've actually done is ensured. They've got behaviors established for each one that gives people clear guidance.

So, for example, courage. What they then explained is if somebody is living the courage value, this is what they'll be doing. You say what you think. Even if it is controversial, you make tough decisions without excessive agonizing. You take smart risks. You question actions inconsistent with our values. In other words, they're actually giving people some behavioral guidance on how to actually live these things. And once you've done that, you can actually start to make them much more tangible. So, again, my experience of this involves others. Getting more people involved will help. I worked with a client where the senior team came up with the core values and the behaviors, but let you send them out there.

And they were under the flood control of the city, and didn't drip down. We talked to some of the guys in different departments and said if somebody was doing this value, what would they be doing? And they described things in their language. They said very, very similar things. But because they use their language and because then we build those into how we did things, they started to own them. So what I'm suggesting here is to get people engaged, and get them to own these things. So the things might be that no one necessarily has published out there. There's things you use internally. So this is what it looked like at our friends at Mudroom Hospice, just to give you a very, very simple example. One of their core values is working together.

So the behavior we came up with is working with the team. Working together means simply demonstrating this value will be contributing positively and proactively to work towards the overall goals of the hospice. That means they're not just working their own team and department, which is something I wanted to emphasize. They'll be taking time to understand the people's roles and functions, and other parts of the organization. We actively encourage people to actually see how other people do things. Sharing knowledge and expertise with others to improve the performance and proactively supporting and acknowledging the contributions of other colleagues.

So what's going on? If you were to spot people doing things well and contributing to making the hospice a positive place to work and visit, see how tangible those things are. You can actually measure people, which is what they've had to do, build into their processes, where you can actually ask people, are they consistently doing this? Occasionally doing this. Rarely doing this. Never doing this. So, again, what I encourage you to do is download the toolkit, work together with other people. You can get them involved in how you can actually shape up the behaviors to reinforce and live the values you've created.

Make It Work For You

So you've established your values. Step one, step two. You made it meaningful. It's now time for step three. And that's about making them work for you and about living them. It's not about nice posters and brochures. It's about what you do and what you do consistently. Back to our friends at Zappos. Value number one is deliver wow through service, which I know sounds very grand and very sort of schmaltzy. If you're not aware that they tell their people to have guidelines, stay on the phone until you get things sorted with a customer. They're a call center. They take calls in their record for the amount of time on a phone for one call is 10 hours, 51 minutes. I'm not suggesting that should be happening all the time. What they're doing, they're creating a war story. But what is also done is making it very clear to people how they want things to be done.

Lots of call centers I work with. One of the key drivers is how to get off the phone as quickly as you can. So what I do here is publish your values and behaviors internally, make them meaningful, train people, reinforce them. Actually, look at how you can build them into your organization. So consider assessing people against the behaviors, both formally or informally. If you are serious about this, one of the things you might want to do is start with the senior people. Start with yourself. How would you rate against these things? I did some work with it with a client. We did exactly that. And we got once we caught up with them, we actually got all the team to recognize and vote and actually assess the leaders, the directors of the business, how they measured up against the values and behaviors.

And the news came in and got them all analyzed. And the financial director scored incredibly low on most of them. And he was absolutely gutted because he had a complete passion for his business. The problem was he walked into the office every morning, said good morning. Everybody went to his office, shut the door and never talked to anybody. He was never seen to be doing these things. So just to start living this, one of the things you might want to do is to start you off by quite symbolically getting people to score and rate you as leaders in terms of how you make this work. But it's about building into your business. And we'll explore these in the following chapters. But think a bit about the recruitment. Think about your H.R. systems and processes, about how you rule and recognize people, work out what you're doing.

But the key thing for me here is you as a role model, do you walk the talk? I was once speaking at a conference or an internal event with a company or about client care and customer care. And the MDA brought me in to speak to all this team. We've got them all in one morning for an hour. And I talked about going the extra mile for customers and how it was vital we did this. And he then said, you heard what everybody said, everybody. This is really what it's all about. Let's make sure we go out there and go the extra mile for customers. It's crucially important we do these things. You then shouted across to his PA in front of his service staff. Gene, if so-and-so rings, tell them in. And I want work that just disappeared like that.

The whole key thing for me here is use this stuff to make it tangible, assess yourself, get others to assess them, and actually start off possibly with the business model of actually getting your employees to do this. So the business I need to work with, we had 270 employees that were actually going to be using this as part of our processes. We actually got them to develop. The assessment tool and actually used it on the directors, on the scene he manages before they do nothing with it. And he showed the company was being very, very open about what's going on. They made it very, very transparent. So this whole idea of valuing your values. I'll show you maybe just how this works.

Scott Harrison, founder, CEO of Charity Water, a brilliant 3D charity that provides fresh water in communities around the world. I'll leave you with his words. I think this is very, very key. He says, putting integrity at the core of everything you do is so much more important than what you do is how you do it. So what are you going to do to establish and use the behaviors you want? So everybody understands them. And it makes them work for you and for your business.

What It Looks Like

This next chapter shares some examples of 3D businesses and how they build systems and processes into their organization. I'm not saying copy them. I'm not trying to give them examples to work out. How are you going to do this stuff in your business? RPM's di köstinger, a precision engineering business. And when they recruit their apprentices, they're looking for people who have attention to detail, can follow instructions and work under pressure two times. So part of the recruitment process is to give them an ethics model. The Spitfire, half an hour to do it, because people can say, I've got to tell you the details. They actually do this not to use it as part of their process to assess people.

When I was working and they gave me a copy of it, I actually left the pilot out of the cockpit. I haven't got the attention to detail to them, but it's a very simple example of a business, I would argue, using something in their recruitment process to maybe reinforce the ethos and the value of the business. Back to Tony. A Zappos quote from him, We interview people for culture fit. We want people who are passionate about what Zappos is about our service. I don't care if they're passionate about shoes. What he wants to know is can they actually look after customers? And they built this into their recruitment process. So, for example, if the taxi company picks you up from the airport to go for the interview, they report back to the recruitment panel what you would like in terms of dealing with them.

I did some work with a client, an engineering business, and the MD told me a story. They were looking for a sales manager and they put an ad to recruit for the sales manager. And this one particular guy turned up for this interview being slothful of you. And it's a bit of a sort of Jack the lad character. He came into reception and he said, oh, I'm here for the interview. The lady said, I'll just sit down there. So he's saying

I said, so what's he like then? The boss here? The receptionist who I love working here. I think it's great. But is he a good lad? Is he OK? Anyway, before she got a chance to answer that, HMDs came through. So do you have to go through to the end? You just sit there for a minute, please. And he sat in the room, sat in his office, and again, he started his chat.

So is he a good bloke, this chap? You know what? We are going to be alright with him. Does he like a few beings? Is he OK? No. At the door of the MDES office opened. When she walked out, she walked out and said, thank you very much. The interview is over. You said you've not questioned me. No, my staff have. They are part of the recruitment process. I do not want somebody in this company working for me who hasn't done any research and who they're going to see and who's making the assumption the MD is a man. Thank you very much. Now, again, I'm not suggesting you've got to start building that into your recruitment processes, but do you recruit people for attitude as well as skills? The Great Escape is an organizational neros, fantastic dynamic business.

And basically, they lock you up in rooms and you have to get out of them as lots around the country. I know Hannah, the M.D., who is doing this business, screwed the business in the early days and recruited people who own likeness. It clearly became a business where people wanted to get involved. So they were bombarded with interview requests and recruitment to be put out for a job. Loads of stuff coming through. It's quite clear lost people weren't up for it. So what they said, well, when we're looking for people who are ambassadors, i.e., people who interact with customers, what we actually want is you to send us a video selling yourself.

So who will I want to do that? Well, if you want to do that, fair chances, you wouldn't be the sort of person we want doing this job in our business. The words they change their recruitment process to actually start helping filter out some of the people that maybe weren't the right fit. And architects practice. I did some work with that in Bristol. I'm one of the things I'd identified when they talked to a lot of employees that the whole idea of client focus wasn't massive. Quite a few people say things I find tough to do with clients and they realize that maybe there were some people who saw themselves as outside people, inside people. So one of the things I did was to start changing what they did.

If you get a job there on your first day, you walk in at nine o'clock by five past nine. You are in a car with a partner going to visit a client regardless of what your job is. You don't see the fire extinguisher. You don't see the fire escapes. You don't see where the coffees and teas made you go out and visit a client. And the message is clients are really important to us. People remember that. It's also quite a good chance for the partner to actually get to know the employee as well. The clients of ours, something we develop with them and for them, call the 30 day health and happiness check. Again, lots of companies I know say things like, oh, it's on the job training or the induction is round, visit everybody. Here's a fire escape. Here's some forms to fill and get on with it.

They really developed their induction because, again, the research shows that very often the time and effort put into recruiting people is wasted if the induction isn't right. But what they do after 30 days, a little questionnaire that you sit down with your boss or with a colleague, I just go through it and basically say things like, are you aware of what's going on in this business? Is the job what you thought it was going to be? How was the recruitment process? Is there anything you do? And it just takes them through this quite systematic, structured way of actually getting people to understand whether they're fitting in, what's going on.

But some questions, things like are there certain things that you've no idea why we do these things? Are there any things you think we could learn from your previous company we could learn from, but also ask, are you aware of what the core values are? And do they mean anything in this business? Again, health and happiness check. It's just something that they used. But again, you can develop that for your business. Martek, a client of ours upon the neck of the woods. Everybody in the team, each team has a full budget, small amount of money that the team can use for social events. They get to spend it how they want, how, because one of their core values is about teamwork, about people. They also have a part of their induction on day one.

When you join the company, an email goes out to the person that everybody else says, this is me, this is my, this is a bit about me and this is my favorite pizza. And they give them their favorite pizza, say, please come to my office, a place where I work, and there's all the pizzas and people just pop in and say hello. It's just a simple way of getting people just to interact. Many people feel welcomed, but actually work out what this means for you. So joining me for a pizza is a very simple little tool and technique. They have to make it work for them. Three Squared are a client that we work with, and they develop software and develop apps. And when they first started, they grew a business.

And every Thursday afternoon, about four o'clock is to stop and have what these called beer knowledge. Thursdays and Benally. It was an hour. Where did you get together with a couple of beers and non-alcoholic drinks were available and just day discuss what was going on. And he knew thoughts and ideas. They've grown massively, very, very successful business, and they've kept that going. It's every month where they bring people together from all customers just to interact alone with each other. Better knowledge. Thursdays work for them. Harley Davidson, every single member of staff that works for Harley

Davidson, has to spend at least two weekends a year at a Harley-Davidson convention interacting with customers.

Whether you're in the finance team, the team from behind the , what to get everybody to get together with their customers. What happens in your business when people leave? Do they just wave goodbye? Do you have any sort of debrief, process and system? And now the end is near. It was a process we developed in our old business when we had sort of 15 employees, but we now usually with our clients. And basically what happens is it's a formal, semi structured discussion. But how was it for you? And again, sometimes we find that some people will say things that they wouldn't normally say if they were still there and a set of questions that you could actually use to find out what people are thinking.

There's even an option. Some clients have done what people can do if they want. It's anonymous. They seal. It doesn't get open till they've left. That's not always the best way of doing things. But I would really encourage you to think a bit about do you have things at the end of the process to actually reinforce the culture and the values you want? Where the business in bestir that I mentioned early on, they actually have an iPad as people walk out of the door and there's some smiling faces. I think it was pressed on how their day to day tends to want to see how things are going. Now, that doesn't give any magic answers. But what Simon says it does from afar, it allows us to keep a track on what MIRALEM motivations like in the business.

So what I mean, could you think a bit about is to look at your systems and processes because they all. Act positively or negatively or neutrally when it comes to reinforcing and supporting your culture. Do yours support and reinforce your culture or do the trapped. So I would like to download the toolkit to help you look at this and then move on to the next chapter where we're going to help you review your systems and processes.

Review And Establish Your Systems

This chapter encourages you to systematically review all your systems and processes because they all act positively or negatively, maybe mutually without I'll give neutral means is probably negatively when it comes to your culture. And this is what I encourage you to do. You'll see the toolkit you can download explains how to do this. But I encourage you to map out the employee journey from somebody first coming to your business. But even first, finding out about your business. So it's a recruitment tool to interview through, to appointment, to induction, to how they're managed and performance development, the communication, how they can get promoted, how they're rewarded and recognized, and also how they're editing. In other words, when you look at these, it allows you to drop them down.

And then we ask you to do, is this be honest? And look, do they actually support and reinforce your culture? How do they do that? You might see it, but all the people think that it is a detriment. So, again, what I would encourage you to do with this one is to actually get the toolkit, do as a team exercise, get other people's thoughts and views. So, for example, you might think that your recruitment process reinforces your ethos. What do the people who've recently joined think? What are the people who've been with you a long time? Are they aware of some of these things that you're talking about? So, in other words, work out whether they act positively or negatively and then identify what steps you need to take to make this stuff work for you.

The Key Steps

Engage, empower and enable. That's the EA of Uber. Now, you'll notice there are a few buzzwords in their engagement empowerment. I was actually once winning a seminar where an M.D. of a quite traditional business came up to me so that one day we'd empower our staff to delight our customers. It turns out when we looked at it five years ago, three wise guys were in a Chamber of Commerce breakfast seminar for 20 minutes on customer service. And that whole ethos to empowerment was almost like you are now empowered. You are now empowered. Empowerment is giving people permission to do things. Engagement is getting bought into this.

And enabling them is actually allowing them and training them and giving the skills to make it work. So engage, empower and enable. And therefore, what we start talking about, this idea of engagement is by creating an establishing passion, purpose and performance in all your people. So some simple things to consider. Have your people bought into your vision? Are they aware of what you're trying to achieve? Do they know what's expected? Have you actually spelt out what your behaviors are? Do they know what they should be doing? I think a great measure of empowerment in a business is what can people do without permission? Timpson is the high street cobblers and key people, every member of Stafford Simpsons is empowered to spend up to five hundred pounds to solve a customer's problem without talking to a manager.

Oh, very often are people spending five hundred pounds, but that's what they're allowed to do. Ritz Carlton Hotels, high end chain of hotels. Every member of staff at the Ritz Carlton is empowered to spend up to two thousand dollars to solve a customer's problem without talking to a manager. And what I'm suggesting here is, is a measure is what can people do in your organization, in your business without having to get permission? And I'm not suggesting it has to be five hundred pounds or two thousand pounds, but do you set clear guidelines? So one of the things I'm sort of suggesting here is what we see in 3-D businesses is that they spell out the behaviors they want, as well as the goals and targets. And again, it's quite exciting when you start looking at this in terms of how it works in the real world.

If we're sort of encouraging people to do this, how does it work? I was asked to do some work with a law firm. And the work I was doing, which was all about client care and managing partner, asked me to spend some time with his teams in different offices to work out what was going wrong with customer service and client care, and what they could do about it. And in the first session, I was doing what I was doing, this training Book. I said to everybody, we want to get your thoughts and views on how we can go, that Samatha clients, when we identify the barriers and anything that you come up with, are going to be sharing back with the managing partner.

This one lady wants to tell you what you start and you start with the partners. So many of them just never answer the phone, never repeat the recall of their clients and consistently get messages. I'll tell you the names of them. And she gave me a list of the top five. I ran these Books in four of the departments and the same names came up. I had to go back to the managing director and managing partner and share with him the feedback and show them the list. He was number two on the list. To be fair to him, he published it. He actually said this is something we will not tolerate in this business anymore. We are spelling out how we want things to be done around here. And one of the things that we will do is that partners will answer calls.

We're going to monotreme. And what was quite interesting was that in the discussion I was with the board at one point and one of them, maybe more I might call established partners, took umbrage to some of these youngsters telling him what to do. And he said, I'm not going to be doing this. And he said this publicly in front of his colleagues. And what was quite interesting, his retirement. We should have it in two years. Time was brought forward by about 18 months. And there's quite a symbolic way of maybe just challenging the challenges. Then people know that we're serious about this stuff. I had another client, bizarrely, another law firm. Well, we actually found all of the challenges in this particular business was that people open plan offices.

People weren't answering other people's phones even though they spelt out. So one of the things that came up with was a very, very simple little method that the managing partner then would ring up. And if you answered the phone, you've got a 50 pound bonus. Now, some people say to me, why would you pay people to do what they should be doing? What is harder to do is to get some of those more resistant to it. Who am I? Give this a go. In other words, it made it part of what they did. So what I'm Covid you think about here is do you champion your champions? Do you spot people doing things? Well, Prettyman, I actually have mystery shoppers who come in and spot people doing things well.

And one of the things they actually have is they actually check whether people are happy and whether they're actually giving great customer service. Looking at how they are, they're doing these things that make people smile, put them on a staff, are allowed to give away a cup of coffee or a sandwich to maybe some people claiming a bad day or regular customer. They're allowed and encouraged to do it. But the mystery shoppers actually come in and they spot people being cheerful. They were cheerful ometer. And if you hit 10 out of 10 for being cheerful on the cheerful amateur, but the mystery shopper exercises, you get a 50 pound bonus because one of their ethos and their values is about teamwork. You have to spend it on and with your colleagues.

I work with another high, high, high profile. I'll tell you the name of a retailer and their staff. Whenever a customer comes into the store, you're going to make eye contact with them within three seconds. That was the rule. Whenever there was news of a mystery shopper or a rumor, Mr. Shopper in town, all you ever saw the staff doing was. To all the customers. What are you measuring? What are you managing? What is rewarding and what are you challenging are the things that will shape the behaviors you actually get from your people. And sometimes these things maybe are seen as being intangible. I was asked to do some work with a financial advisor, and the MD asked me to spend some time with the people, find out what's going on, get a feel of what's going on.

And I went back to him and said, you've got a real problem. This guy is called Colin. Well. Colin was one of their financial advisers four days a week, he was out on the road dealing with clients, leaving customers one day a week on a Friday to come in, do his paperwork, and people told me that Colin was quite aggressive, quite pushy. We actually found when we started talking about him, something's going on. So I said to this guy, you have a real problem with Colin. He said, have you seen Colin's targets? Let me tell you the pain that doesn't lie, cause you're right. But what isn't on your panel is the fact that I've identified at least three people who've left because of Colin. I've actually got evidence that absenteeism is higher on a Friday when he's not in. I've actually got stories. I can't prove it.

But I've heard people say that if we're getting toward the end of the month and colleagues offer a big target, paperwork goes missing. So he didn't achieve his target that month. But clients don't get what they want and need either. None of those are on your panel. So we invited Colin in. And to be fair to the guy, he was absolutely gutted. What he thought was enthusiasm and getting him to was actually seen as being bullying aggressive by what else? He went out with the MDY. And I was totally sad. And he said, stop if it's an apology. And said, if you ever see you do this again, please, I know I'm not going to make someone who is scared of me, talk to me, tell him.

And he publicly admitted he got things wrong and he changed his behaviors. Now, that doesn't happen all the time. But what really could you think about if you're looking at this whole idea of empowering, engaging and enabling people? How do you measure up? Do you actually make this stuff work and you make it tangible in your organization? Have a look at the next chapter and we'll give you some tools and techniques to actually make this work for you and for your business.

Get It Right In Your Business

This chapter encourages you to take a bit of time out and to review your approach. As we've mentioned, when we start looking at the things that are happening in your organization, all these things that we've talked about, and positively or negatively or neutrally when it comes to your culture and what you will see in the toolkit is a set of guidelines to work on and just work your way through it. Have a look at what the key issues are in your organization. More importantly, do something with them and actually make sure that you are working out what you need to do to engage, enable and empower your people to make these things work for you.

Making Rewards And Recognition Work For You

What do you reward and recognize in your business? And I mean, formally or informally, what I mean by this is that the things that you reward and recognize will often shape the behaviors that people actually demonstrate. I was working with a client and she was saying to me, as the MDC said, I'm really struggling to get my people to go the extra mile for our clients. And I said, well, what do they get if they do that? She said, what do you mean? I said, what do people get if they actually go to that swath of clients? She goes, they don't get anything. I said, they do. She goes, What? I said, they get more work. The rewards are a great job as you get to do more. If I would even suggest that those that don't do these things, get away with it. But the words you are informally rewarding people for doing a great job by giving them more work to do.

And therefore, what I'm suggesting when you start looking at this is to start working out what are the things that you reward and recognize people for in your organization? The research suggests that 79 percent of employees say that recognition tied to core values gives them a stronger sense of the company's goals and objectives. In other words, this is not just about hitting targets with one particular client, where for a long, long time the only people ever got rewarded with big sales guys to live in these great contracts. But actually, the MDY, he was telling me when he thought about it, he said, you know, the people who choose the proposals, the people who support them will do nothing to them.

So what we actually introduced was a methodology within the business that anybody could be highlighted by somebody else in the business for doing a great job in line with the values of the organization. In other words, do you actually have reward mechanisms not just for hitting goals and targets, but for living the behaviors that we've been talking about? I keep talking about law firms. I did some work with a law firm. But one of the things that they identified was that some things sometimes went wrong with clients. And the managing partner came with this idea called the cockup fund. And the cockup fund was a budget that anybody could tap into to say sorry to a client if it happened, if something had gone wrong, whether you wanted to send him a bottle of wine, a bunch of flowers, a box of chocolates, whatever it might be.

And he launched it to say, look, just to sort of encourage people to do this there for the first two months. It wasn't touched. Nobody went anywhere near it. And he actually saw people do it. Are you telling me in the last two months we've done nothing? That's gone wrong. And actually what we found was and I can understand it, people will actually admit that they got things wrong. So what they actually created was a bit bizarre. We actually created a key indicator. They actually wanted people to spend the money not to do things wrong, but just to get out the openness of actually how we want people to admit things have gone wrong. How we knew something about it.

So what we're saying here is, do we actually reward people for getting things wrong? No. Do we reward people for admitting it and doing something about it? Southwest Airlines. They actually have a very simple process where their customers. Spot staff doing things well, and they can actually feel a little formally handed in and the staff can actually use them and claim prizes for them. So they've actually got their customers spotting the champions of things, doing things well, benchmark recruits, a client of ours, and they have a thing called votes of values. And what that is, is only a small team, but anybody and everybody can just recognize other colleagues who've done something in line with the values of the organization. And they put the name in little John at the end of the month.

That is, bring these all things together and actually just encourage people to just share what's going on. And. People might think it's a bit touchy feely. They measure people and manage people and hitting targets. They also measure amongst people for living the values, our friends at Rotherham Hospice. One of the things that they have is that you can actually mock somebody and mugging somebody is basically you somebody in the team or something particularly well, you fill a mug with things that they like. So if they like sweets and chocolates, you put sweets and chocolates. And if they like fruit, it's just a very simple way of just acknowledging people. But a little note saying thanks very much for doing this.

Another great example was when I was in Morison's supermarket chain and went into where we normally shop. And the lady who looked after us, who often looks afterwards in lots of different ways when we have a go. She was saying to us, she said to my wife, Jill, Jill, have you seen my name? What? My name's on the board. And at the back of the supermarket was a big board that said what our customers thought. And customers have been encouraged to write down little things about members of staff that have gone the extra mile, and have done things. And her name was on there, that Pam did a fantastic job. So we went and we were giving it a thumbs up. And she was beaming.

We wrote one stall on that. Well. She was beaming, even double. I'm not saying it's just about putting signs on notice boards. What I'm saying here is do we actually acknowledge and accept that there are people doing things good, doing things well, and that we can actually champion those people? So reward and recognition doesn't have to be lots of shiny amounts of money. It just could be acknowledgement, one word of warning in terms of how you actually reward and recognize people. I was in a big out of town shopping center and I had these posters up, said, please nominate our customer champions in this men's outfit shop. And these young ladies that serve me, I called Brett, were outstanding and I said, I'm nominating you.

You know, please don't. I said, why not? World had seven nominations this month, so that's great, you'll win because I don't want to win. Why not? Because the prize you get to go to dinner with the managing director if you're going to reward and recognize people. Make sure it's in line with something that works for them. So when we start talking about reward and recognition, it doesn't have to be about lots of money. What I'm saying here is, have you got things in your organization, in your business that reinforces the behaviors you actually want? What do you reward and recognize formally and informally in your business? Look at the next chapter and just get a feel for what you need to do to make this work for you.

How To Make It Work For You

So we've talked about rewarding and recognizing people. What I would encourage you to do, download the toolkit, but ask people in your team, what do we reward and recognize around here? Both formally and this is a key one. Informally, what are the things that we actually reward and recognize people for? And again, you might find some inconsistencies here, some key issues that might come out that you didn't realize. People are being rewarded for doing the wrong things. But also it includes you thinking about this. What do we tolerate that maybe we shouldn't? One of the things you sometimes find is that your culture is often a reflection of the things you tolerate, not only in a negative way of looking at this, but I would really encourage you to say the certain things that people do.

The people can get away with it, if I'm honest. Very often at senior level. So what I encourage you to think about here is take some time out. Use a tool kit to work out. What do you do to reward and recognize things formally, informally? What do you tolerate? What do you need to do to actually make sure that you're rewarding and recognizing the behaviors you want?

Conclusion

Let's have a look back at some of the things we've talked about and we talked about, our definition of culture has been the way we do things around here positively and negative, and will encourage you to work out which aspects of your culture you're happy with, you're not happy with what other people think. We introduced the whole concept of OBOR culture. Everybody understands what's expected of them and behaves consistently in line with that. Your systems and processes are built to reinforce those behaviors. People are engaged, empowered and enabled to make them work, and they're rewarded and recognized for doing so either formally or informally. So Cuba is a model. I would encourage you to do the assessment again. At least that's what you did right at the beginning.

And actually, you might find this perhaps a bit bizarre. You actually might find that you've actually scored it lower now, because I've amplified the pain a little bit and maybe showed you what it could be like, but as ever. Download the toolkit and work out what it is you need to do to create an uber culture in your business. So there was an uber culture development plan. Download that and use it to work out what your next steps are going to be. Have a go. Some milestones. Engage people. Get people involved in this to make it work for you. I would even suggest that the way you go about doing this than itself will shape the culture of your business. Dan Machala, co-founder of HubSpot, says you're going to have a culture anyway. You can and should influence it. So why not build the one you love? What you enjoy doing.

Creating Your Plan And Your Next Steps

Hopefully, you're now on a path to creating the culture that you actually want. But what I thought I just let you do is to know that there are other Books via Experts Academy to actually help you do these things. We've got some Books on leadership and on business performance. So the Books are worth looking at. How do you actually live your role as a leader? How do you actually get that vision? How do you get people on board? Reinforce some of the things we talked about in this one. Employee engagement does the same. How do you actually get your people on board to make some of these happen? These things happen and deliver what they should be doing.

There is a Book on marketing, finding, attracting and keeping the customers that you want. There's one on maximizing customer relationships, how to get the best to get the best from the customers you actually want. All these things, I would argue your culture will help shape and intertwine with these things. So they are all linked. Please get in touch with any questions, queries, any successes you've had. You can contact me by household income filing 10 via Facebook and Twitter. And all I say is have a go. Go for it. Win is to take action. Not notes. Make it work for you and all the best.

Don't miss out!

Visit the website below and you can sign up to receive emails whenever SADANAND PUJARI publishes a new book. There's no charge and no obligation.

https://books2read.com/r/B-A-YJFBB-FZDYC

BOOKS2READ

Connecting independent readers to independent writers.

Also by SADANAND PUJARI

Master The Psychology Of Weight Loss Via Hypnosis Build Healthy
Sleep Habits Learn The Art Of Meditation
Improve People Management And Build Employee Engagement
Content Marketing Masterclass Create Content That Sells
Cyber Security For Normal People Protect Yourself Online
Kanban Fundamentals How To Become Insanely Productive
Positive Psychology Art Therapy: Certified Training
Bookkeeping In Quickbooks Online (Bookkeeping & Accounting)
Business Impact of Digital Transformation Technologies